Petra Sophia Zimn

111 Places
in Verona
and Lake Garda
That You
Must Not Miss

emons:

For Alba and Stella

© Emons Verlag GmbH
All rights reserved
© Photographs: Petra Sophia Zimmermann, except
page 63: Grand Hotel a Villa Feltrinelli; page 143: Marco Calliari;
page 207: Petra Sophia Zimmermann, with kind permission
of the Museo di Castelvecchio
Design: Eva Kraskes, based on a design
by Lübbeke | Naumann | Thoben
Maps: altancicek.design, www.altancicek.de
English translation: Alan Gentile
Editor: Katrina Fried
Printing and binding: Grafisches Centrum Cuno, Calbe
Printed in Germany 2015
ISBN 978-3-95451-611-7
First edition

Did you enjoy it? Do you want more?
Join us in uncovering new places around the world on:
www.111places.com

Foreword

It's vacation at first sight as you cross over the Alps and catch your first glimpse of heavenly Lake Garda, with its endlessly long banks. You immediately begin to imagine swimming in the crystal-clear water and savoring the long last sliver of the sun as it sets behind the dock of a picturesque village along the Riviera degli Olivi (the Olive Riviera). But Lake Garda beckons with much more than just the *dolcefarniente* – the quintessential Italian pastime of taking pleasure in relaxing.

This guidebook will open your eyes to 111 must-see attractions around Lake Garda and Verona. Did you know, for example, that the Riva yachts so famous here actually have nothing to do with the town of Riva del Garda, on the north end of the lake? That on the western shore, lemons were being sculpted into the capitals of columns in the 13th century, but that the town of Limone has nothing to do with the bitter fruit?

The deep blue of the lake and the yellow of the lemons grown on its shores are reflected in the colors found on the coat of arms of Verona – a city whose location and history have tied it closely to Lake Garda. For tourists, Verona is best known as the city of the most famous and tragic lovers in the world, Romeo and Juliet, and of the ancient Roman arena with its annual opera festival. But have you ever heard the true story of Juliet's famous balcony? Or the circumstances surrounding the 13th-century "Casa di Romeo"– the house in which the handsome young suitor could very well have lived? And do you know where to find the tastiest tarts in the city, or where the sweet *pandoro* cake is immortalized in stone?

This book will lead you to 111 special places rarely mentioned in conventional travel guides, but which lend this history-laden idyll its sensual magic. We'll echo the cheerful locals when we wish you *Buon divertimento!*: Have fun and enjoy!

111 Places

1_ Cantina Zeni

Learning and tasting in the museum of wine

Situated just a mile or so from central Bardolino, the prestigious Cantina Zeni is well signposted and easy to find. For more than twenty years, the Zeni family has run a *museo del vino*, or wine museum, on the grounds of their renowned winery, which was founded in 1870. The museum showcases different grape varietals and has historical winemaking equipment on display, such as hand mills, a *mostarola*, or press, and a wooden cask in which the grapes were once mashed by foot in the style of Lucille Ball. Today the production process is fully mechanized, and visitors can also view the modern bottling plant.

The Zeni family owns five vineyards in the picturesque province of Verona. On 62 acres around Bardolino, they grow the red grapes that go into the smooth Bardolino DOC Classico and the more up-scale Bardolino Classico Superiore DOCG. Their rosé, Chiaretto Classico Vigne Alte, in which the white juice from the grapes is separated from their red skins after only 24 hours, leaving the wine a lighter, more copper-colored hue, was recently named the best in the world.

Proud siblings Fausto, Elena, and Federica Zeni have also unveiled a new "natural" wine lacking in the usual sulfites. They have been working on its development for a full six years. This red, named I Filari del Nino, is dedicated to the memory of their late father, Nino.

The guided winery tour takes you through the *bottaia*, a huge vaulted cellar with barrels stretching as far as the eye can see. How long the wine is aged and the type of wood the barrel is made from help determine the variety of wine produced. It is either here or in the museum itself where the wine tastings take place. You can sample and buy the famous reds along with the other products of Cantina Zeni, such as the fresh white wine produced in the region or the reds produced in Valpolicella.

Address Cantina Fratelli Zeni Srl, Via Costabella 9, 37011 Bardolino (VR), Tel 0039/045/7210022 | **Getting there** From the Gardesana Orientale (SR249), signs will guide you to the road up into the hills leading to the wine museum. | **Hours** Mar 18 – Oct 31, daily 9am – 1pm and 2:30 – 7pm. For winter hours, call or send an email to museodelvino@zeni.it. | **Tip** Cantina Zeni sponsors and serves their wines at the Concerti del Venerdì, classical concerts held annually over four Fridays in August and September in Bardolino.

2 La Conchiglia

A slice of heaven thanks to Pino

Pino knows everyone in Bardolino. For around 20 years he's run his restaurant here, where patrons crowd the tables set under the large fans inside, on the patio, or along the front of the building. Pino, the *pizzaiuolo*, or pizza maker – whose real name is Giuseppe Conti – has won various awards over the years and in 2013 took home not only the title of Pizza World Champion, but was also crowned "Olympic Champion 2013" at the Pizza Olympics. Little wonder then that he moonlights as a professor at the Scuola Italiana Pizzaiuoli (the Italian School of Pizza).

When asked the secret to his success, he replies simply, *Lavorare con amore* – he works with love. For him, the best pizza is still the classic pizza margherita, with tomatoes, buffalo mozzarella, and fresh basil. For his sauce, he uses only the special small tomatoes known as *pomodori pacchino*.

Pizza margherita takes its name from Queen Margherita, the wife of Italy's King Umberto I. In 1889, she was presented this masterpiece by a Neapolitan baker and chose it as her favorite, not just for its symphony of flavors, but also because its green, white, and red colors represented those found on the Italian flag. The pizza was thereafter named in her honor.

La Conchiglia's menu includes many other dishes, but most patrons come for one of the 67 varieties of pizza on offer. Beyond these, there are an infinite number of possibilities for diners, since you can truly personalize a pie in any way you can imagine by choosing your own combination of toppings. Plus: each day, new and creative specials come out of the oven. There is also the Pizza Panara Mista, which will satisfy the whole family.

Cutlery is provided, but guests are encouraged to eat their pizza with their hands – the Italian way. Pino's aromatic and delicious pies can't properly be described on paper, however – they must be tasted to be truly appreciated.

Address Borgo Garibaldi 19, 37011 Bardolino (VR), Tel 0039/045/7210603 | **Getting there** From SR 249 follow signs to designated parking areas, as the city center is a pedestrian zone. | **Hours** Mar–Oct, Mon–Sun until late in the evening; open in the winter months depending on demand | **Tip** In addition to La Conchiglia's main restaurant in Bardolino, there are now three offshoots including a pizzeria in Verona right behind the Arena on Via Leoncino.

3 Festa dell'Uva e del Vino
A festival of wine tasting

The construction of fantastic structures on the rocks along the waterfront is a telltale sign that it's once again that time of year: the Festa dell'Uva e del Vino (Grape and Wine Festival) is coming.

For more than 80 years between late September and early October, Bardolino has celebrated *la vendemmia*, or grape harvest, with a grand party that takes over the town. Over five days, Bardolino's vintners set up stalls along the lakeside promenade, even spilling over the shoreline, pouring out their wine for festival goers to taste and savor.

The locals organize the celebration for the many visitors who come to the area specifically for the harvest. As with many other regional festivals throughout Italy, it's also a great opportunity to try local gastronomic specialties alongside your glass of wine, such as the classic risotto or seafood and meat with polenta. Actors dressed in historical costumes, music, theater, and fireworks all enhance the event.

Of course, it is also an opportunity for the more than 60 wineries in and around Bardolino to proudly show off the high-quality ruby-red wine that is named after their hometown.

Bardolino is the "controlled designation of origin," or *Denominazione di origine controllata* (DOC), of this variety of wine, done to ensure that high-quality standards are met consistently. For the finest wines produced here, the wine is classified as "controlled designation of origin guaranteed," or DOCG. The grapes going into the wine must therefore come from Bardolino or its well-defined environs, be pressed there, and bottled on-site. In addition, the ratio of types of grapes that go into the red wine and the copper-hued rosé Chiaretto is strictly defined: Corvina Veronese and Rondinella make up the majority, with at most 20 percent coming from other varieties, such as Molinara, Rossignola, Merlot, or Cabernet Sauvignon.

Address Lungolago Riva Cornicello and Piazza del Porto, 37011 Bardolino (VR) |
Getting there From the Gardesana (SR 249), follow the signs to the town parking
lots. | **Hours** The festival runs for five days at the end of Sep/beginning of Oct.
Information and exact dates can be obtained from the Fondazione Bardolino Top,
Piazza Matteotti 8, 37011 Bardolino (VR), Tel 0039/045/6212586,
www.bardolinotop.it | **Tip** Wineries along the "Strada del Vino" can be visited
all year long. For information, visit Piazza Matteotti 8, 37011 Bardolino (VR),
Tel 0039/045/6212567, www.bardolino-stradadelvino.it.

4 The Harborside Sales Counter

The fishing village and its sister city

The sign welcoming you to Bardolino shows you two interesting facets of the city. First, it refers to one of its most important traditional industries by pointing out that the town gave its name to the blend of red wine produced here. Beneath that, it reads, "twin with Rednitzhembach." During the summer of 2004, Bardolino formed a sister-city partnership with Rednitzhembach, a community of 7,000 high in Germany. As with many places along Lake Garda, the high rates of postwar tourism helped establish these "twin" city exchanges, in this case with assistance from the Bavarian government. Some suspect, though, that Rednitzhembach, in northern Bavaria, was really only chosen to give the Italians a lesson in proper German pronunciation.

It is here among the rolling hills on the eastern shore of the lake that the people have made their living in agriculture and the production of wine and olive oil. Even today, the area south of Bardolino is characterized by wide, undulating vineyards and olive groves. Going back in time, however, fishing also played an important role in the region's economy. We're reminded of this by a massive table made of pink marble along the harborfront, where local fishermen once sold their fresh catch in the early-morning hours.

Though today you're only likely to see a handful of small colorful fishing boats bobbing alongside the many sailboats and motorboats in the large harbor, Bardolino still manages to preserve the character of an old, lively fishing village. It may be due to the unimpeded views of the lake from all points in the village center, unavailable in many of the other small hilly towns bordering this stretch of the shore. The long, wide promenade along the lake also contributes to the unspoiled vistas and to the feeling that visitors can better mingle with locals.

Address At the harborfront, Lungolago Francesco Lenotti, 37011 Bardolino (VR) | **Getting there** From the SR 249, signs will guide you to town parking lots. | **Tip** Since early 2014, Bardolino has held a "Bierfest," where you can sample the beer brewed at one of the breweries in Rednitzhembach.

5 __ San Zeno
The church in the courtyard

The church of San Zeno in Bardolino is a hidden jewel waiting to be discovered. The building dates from the Carolingian period and its first mention goes back to the year 807, when it was described as being under the jurisdiction of the powerful Benedictine abbey of San Zeno in Verona.

As one of the oldest buildings found in Italy – from the time of Charlemagne – San Zeno is fascinating for the fact that both its original ninth-century construction and fragments of the original art – such as the Virgin Mary sitting on the throne holding her child – survive.

A gateway leads you into the Corte San Zeno, a courtyard where the small holy structure stands to the left. The simple houses surrounding the church, which join together to form the round courtyard, were built much later.

From the outside, the only clue that this is a religious building is the bell hanging in one of the higher walls. This makes the interior dimension and shape of the church unexpected and almost surprising. The building was built in the shape of the Latin cross, with the short aisles penetrating a long nave. A high, cross-vaulted tower rises over the intersection.

Six strong red marble columns dating from ancient times were reused in the construction of the church. They are found in the closed arcades of the side walls and in front of the rectangular choir box, and therefore serve no structural purpose, but are simply decorative. Only one of the ancient Ionic capitals was available, however; it can be seen on the column just to the right of the altar. This original capital was probably used as the template for a copy carved out of stone on the column across the way. The attempt at a reproduction was not entirely successful, however, as the spiral scroll of the newer capital is not level, and the rest of the ornamentation is somewhat poorly replicated.

Address Via S. Zeno 13–15, 37011 Bardolino (VR) | **Getting there** From the Gardesana (SR249), Via San Zeno leads directly to the church. | **Hours** Usually open during the day | **Tip** The small town of San Zeno di Montagna is also named after the patron saint of Verona, and is worth a visit for its unique panoramic view of Lake Garda.

6__ The Centomiglia

The legendary regatta

Tranquil Bogliaco is a bastion for sailing. On weekends, you can pinpoint the location of the village from far across the lake, simply based on the number of sailboats bobbing about, and in the warmer months there are numerous sailing races held here. The historic Circolo Vela Gargnano sailing club organizes many of these competitions, including the famous Centomiglia, one of the world's largest regattas held on an inland body of water.

Since it began in 1951, the Centomiglia has taken place annually on the second weekend in September, and the event attracts not only sportsmen but also numerous spectators to Bogliaco and Lake Garda. Centomiglia, which means "one hundred miles" in Italian, pays homage to the famous 1,000-mile Mille Miglia auto race held each year from Brescia to Rome, and the sailing course traverses the lake for 100 miles.

On the morning of the race, visitors crowd around to marvel at the 130 to 300 boats and yachts of different approved classes, arranging themselves between the two buoys marking the starting line. Anyone crossing the line before the cannon shot announcing the commencement of the race is disqualified.

The course begins by running north until the buoy at Torbole, when the wind shifts and the strong southerly *Ora* fills the sails. It then heads towards the southern end of the lake to Desenzano, and turns back toward the starting point, where the lead boats usually finish around 4pm. Meanwhile, numerous vendors set up stalls along the lakeshore, open until the wee hours, creating a lively and jovial atmosphere.

The European sailing season officially comes to an end with the Centomiglia each year, and many boats are subsequently pulled out of the water for the winter. The winning boats can be seen later along the quays, proudly wearing their bib numbers and medals on their bows.

Address Circolo Vela Gargnano, Via Alessandro Bettoni 23, 25084 Gargnano (BS), Tel 0039/0365/71433, www.centomiglia.it | **Getting there** Take the SS 45 into the center of Bogliaco; parking lots are well marked. Parking can also be found at the harbor. | **Tip** The 18th-century Villa Bettoni, stretching north from the harbor along the lake, deserves a look. The Gardesana Occidentale runs directly between its front and its beautifully landscaped Italianate gardens.

7__ The Aril

One of the shortest rivers in the world

In the old fishing village of Cassone di Malcesine, you get the impression that time has stood still. Fishermen bob about in the harbor in their colorful boats. An old round tower marks the entrance to the harbor from Lake Garda.

The village is especially known for the small river that runs through it. A placard on the main street proudly proclaims in four languages that with its 175 meters, the Aril is the shortest river in the world. In truth, the Roe River in the US state of Montana takes the prize, at just sixty-one meters long. Many will assure you, however, that when it comes to picturesque settings, the Aril truly has no competition.

In summer and when the rains are sparse, the Aril carries little water. Those living along its banks can't let their guard down, however, as after a good rainfall the river rises powerfully and swiftly from the earth.

When this happens, a basin alongside the river, or *laghetto* as it's known to the locals, catches the overflow and prevents flooding. The fact that this small river powered a flour mill in earlier times speaks to the force that it can carry. It flows over a waterfall and is crossed by three bridges before gushing into Lake Garda.

The Aril is an environmentally protected waterway, as trout swim up from the lake to spawn here. At one time, a fish farm was headquartered in a building alongside the harbor. Since 2008, this same building has housed the Museo del Lago (Lake Museum). Visitors get an up-close look at a traditional fishing boat and historical tools of the trade. Among the display cases you'll also find an example of the impressive jaws of a *luccio*, or pike, a predatory fish known for its about 700 teeth.

Outside are two pools full of Aril water holding the fish of the region, such as *corregone* (a native whitefish), *trota* (trout), and *anguilla* (eel).

Address 37018 Cassone di Malcesine (VR) | **Getting there** The Gardesana Orientale SR249 runs right through Cassone. There is typically no problem finding parking throughout the village. | **Hours** Museo del Lago, Apr–Sep, Tues–Sun 10am–12pm and 3–6pm. For winter opening times email info@malcesinepiu.it. | **Tip** There are a handful of inviting restaurants along the lakefront.

8 Museo dell'Olio d'Oliva
A lesson in "liquid gold"

When many visitors conjure up visions of the shores of Lake Garda, the first image that comes to mind is the terraces of lemon trees on the western lakefront, which give that area its nickname, the *Riviera dei Limoni* ("Lemon Riviera"). Across the lake, however, you'll find a slightly different topography, which lends itself well to the cultivation of olives. That has garnered a new moniker for this eastern shore, the *Riviera degli Olivi*, or "Olive Riviera."

It makes sense, then, that the Museo dell'Olio d'Oliva (Museum of Olive Oil) would be found here in the small village of Cisano, part of the municipality of Bardolino. The cubic, dark-bricked building, located directly on the Gardesana, does not hark back to an old oil mill as one might expect, however, but rather was specially designed in 1988 by the oil producer Umberto Turri as a museum with a tasting room and shop. Today it is run by his son Flavio and his wife, Liliana Martino.

The exhibition lays out before you the entire olive oil production process in this most northerly olive-producing region in the world. A film, offered in multiple languages, describes the historic sequence of steps in the making of olive oil, including the use of presses, mills, and tools, and compares them with the mechanized systems used today. What's most interesting is that, regardless of whether powered by donkey, water, steam, or electricity, the actual technique of olive-oil production has remained greatly unchanged for centuries.

The highlight of the tour is certainly the tasting, and you'll appreciate the "liquid gold" all the more when you realize that production requires year-round work on the olive plantations, and that it takes more than thirty pounds of olives to produce just one liter of oil.

Various grades of olive oil are available for sampling, including some from other regions of Italy, and all products are offered for sale.

Address Via Peschiera 54, 37011 Cisano di Bardolino (VR), Tel 0039/045/6229047, www.museum.it | **Getting there** Onsite parking is available off the SR 249. | **Hours** Mon–Sat, 9am–12:30pm and 2:30–7pm; Sun, 9am–12:30pm; call for group appointments | **Tip** A quick detour off the main road will take you to a spot just above the museum to see the beautiful olive tree plantations.

9__ Villa dei Cedri
The spa in the park

The Parco Termale del Garda in Colà di Lazise does not count itself among the *parchi del Garda* (amusement parks of Lake Garda) that you'll see signposted all over the region. In contrast to Gardaland, Sealife, Movieland Park, Adventure Park, and the other theme parks that attract huge crowds of tourists around Lazise and Peschiera, Parco Termale is a beautifully landscaped garden and historic site – which happens to also include thermal lakes, pools, and fountains situated among rare plants and ancient trees.

The small town of Colà lies atop a hill and is dominated by the extensive Villa dei Cedri estate. Beginning in 1989, the complex was broken up and repurposed; the villa itself, a magnificent neoclassical structure, is now used as a hotel, and various outbuildings have been remodeled into vacation rentals and apartments. This includes the 16th-century Villa Moscardo, which now houses an elegant upscale restaurant.

In 1989, while drilling for the groundwater that would be used in the irrigation system for the grounds, workers hit the source of the thermal water now used for the spa. The water, which springs from a depth of over 500 feet and reaches a temperature of nearly 100 degrees Fahrenheit (37 degrees Celsius), is channeled into the basin of a former lake to use as a thermal bath. Today about 3,500 cubic meters of mineral-rich water gushes up from the ground daily, replacing nearly half of the volume of the old lake.

The public bathing area is entered through a small neo-Gothic gatehouse. From here, the stunning gardens spread out over 32 acres. Rolling lawns are dotted with old trees, among them nearly 150 cedar trees, or *cedri*, which give the park its name.

Lawn chairs are scattered about, and you're free to lounge or take a soothing dip in the waters – recommended especially for those with skin problems – until after midnight. Hydromassage is also available in the spectacularly lit lake grotto.

Address Piazza di Sopra 4, 37010 Colà di Lazise (VR), Tel 0039/045/7590988, www.villadeicedri.it | **Getting there** The road to Colà branches south off the SR 249 from Lazise. There is a large parking lot in front of the Parco Termale. | **Hours** In Summer, Mon– Fri and Sun 9am–1am, Sat 9am–2am; from mid-Oct, Mon–Thurs, 9am–9pm, Fri and Sun 9am–11pm, Sat 9am–2am; call for winter hours. | **Tip** Combine a visit to the baths with a stop in Lazise, a picturesque walled town with impressive battlements and a castle dating from the rule of the Scala family.

10 __ The German War Cemetery

A seemingly endless graveyard

The German War Cemetery, or Deutsche Soldatenfriedhof, sits atop a hill in the south of Costermano. At the entrance, a sign in German reads, "In this cemetery rest more than 20,000 soldiers and other casualties of war. Their graves remind the living of the harm of war. Their deaths urge us to keep the peace." Just one look at the endless rows of tombstones covering the terraced grounds will send shivers down your spine.

The German War Graves Commission created the Costermano cemetery (the third largest in Italy) and its simple chapel between 1955 and 1967, and it maintains the site on behalf of the German government. Buried here are German soldiers and other casualties of war killed in northern Italy during World War II, especially in its final two years.

After Benito Mussolini was overthrown and the Kingdom of Italy declared war against the German Reich in October 1943, the Wehrmacht successfully took control of many parts of Italy. With increasing brutality, the occupying forces fought against the Italian Resistance, an insurgency and liberation movement made up completely of antifascist groups, and oftentimes the civilian population found itself in the crosshairs, becoming victims of the violent occupation. In its way, the cemetery at Costermano only puts one side of the story on display. It does point out, however, that among the 22,000 soldiers buried, there are some who are responsible for war crimes such as the killing of innocent civilians.

Most of the gravestones are inscribed with the names, ranks, and dates of birth and death of the interred, though you'll see some marked only *"ein deutscher Soldat"* ("a German soldier"). There are plenty of places to sit, reflect, and take in the panoramic views of Lake Garda.

Address Via Baesse 12, 37010 Costermano (VR) | Getting there Follow signs for the German War Cemetery on the SP 8, which runs between Garda and the highway feeder road SP 9. | Hours Mon–Sun 8am–6pm | Tip A quick car ride down the SP 9 will bring you to Locanda San Verolo, an atmospheric restaurant with an outdoor terrace and hotel in an old manor house.

11 The Studio of Pino Castagna

Huge sculptures you just can't miss

As you drive by Costermano on the Via Salita degli Olivi, the road that connects Garda to the highway, it becomes very clear, very quickly, that a larger-than-life artist dwells nearby.

Pino Castagna's studio, which he founded here in 1969 and has since enlarged several times, is marked by rudimentary wooden stelae from the artist's early creative period. While these sculptures are constantly on display in front of the low studio building, other temporary exhibits dot the landscape. Again and again, the pieces are moved and rearranged around the property, and some find their way off the property altogether and straight into the hands of collectors.

A good portion of the expansive grounds abuts the winding road, and you're impelled to slow down and take in the art at the proper Italian pace. Your gaze will pass among the renowned sculptor's works, including *Orogenesi* or *La Nascita delle Montagne* (The Birth of the Mountains), which has a width of about 62 feet. Resembling newly formed layers of rock, curved elements build and stack in rows, rising off the base. Each element is made up of two weathering-steel plates filled with concrete to resemble a mountain peak. Other works by the artist, similarly dealing with the dynamics of the earth and the elements, can now be seen in prominent public places all over the world.

Castagna's pieces can also be viewed in his hometown of Garda. In the entrance to the city hall, his *Canneto*, or reeds, stretch over 20 feet into the air. The bundle of blue Murano glass tubes is inspired by bamboo, in that each tube is created from many similar segments piled on one another. In the gardens behind the hall you can see two more of his pieces: *Donna Incinta* (Pregnant Woman), an aluminum sculpture dating from 1969, as well as *Due Figure* (Two Figures), a sculpture made out of fire clay in 1970.

Address Via Salita degli Olivi 20, 37010 Costermano (VR), Tel 0039/045/7200116 |
Getting there From the end of the SS 450 in Affi, the road to Garda leads through
Costermano; the way to Costermano is also marked from the SR 249 in Garda. | **Tip**
You can pick up beautiful ceramics by Pino Castagna suitable for everyday use in a
shop at Calle dei Sottoportici 14–16 in Garda.

12__ Villa Romana
A floor full of fishing cherubs

Late antiquity saw an economic crisis come over Italy, which caused many citizens to leave the big cities and resettle on rural lands, building magnificent estates that we see today as the villas. There were a handful of Roman villas scattered around Lake Garda, such as those in Desenzano and Sirmione, and over on the western shore in Toscolano-Maderno.

Villa Romana, situated on a beautiful spot right along the lakeshore in Desenzano, is one unique example. According to research performed on the history of the site, there was a structure there dating back to the 1st century A.D. that was subsequently expanded, and fundamentally rebuilt in the first half of the 4th century. Excavations on an area of about 2.5 acres brought to light the estate with its grand villa and a handful of outbuildings.

Floor plans on information boards dotted around the site provide visitors with a good orientation of the complex as they move about the ruins atop a boardwalk.

The main building is especially fascinating, as the succession of rooms with their furnishings, hypocaust heating system, and the remaining fragments of the mosaic flooring display the luxurious lifestyle of the residents over 1,500 years ago.

Among the multicolored mosaics with figural representations, the eye can't help but be drawn to two areas in one of the living quarters, in which two girls and two cherubs are braiding garlands of flowers and fruit. The most unique piece of decorative tilework, however, is that found in the entryway of the villa, where winged cherubs are shown fishing, either sitting in small gondola-like boats as they hold their lines in the water, or standing on the rocks throwing baitfish from their baskets. The scenes depicted don't provide much information about the house or its inhabitants, but the proximity of Lake Garda certainly had something to do with the choice of motif.

Address Via Crocefisso 22, 25015 Desenzano del Garda (BS) | Getting there The villa can be reached from the SS 572; there is a public parking lot immediately nearby (entrance on Via Antonio Gramsci). | Hours Mar–Oct, Tues–Sun 8:30am–7:30pm; Nov–Feb, Tues–Sun 8:30am–5pm | Tip You can't miss *The Last Supper* by Gian Battista Tiepolo found in the sacrament chapel of the Desenzano cathedral located nearby in town.

13 Baia delle Sirene

A picture-postcard beach

Lake Garda has such a long coastline that you would think finding a sandy beach with great swimming and access to the water would be easy. Beaches, however, are few and far between. There are a handful of places with small pebble beaches, and you can find several patches of green dotted with lawn chairs between the busy coastal road and the water. A unique exception to this is the Baia delle Sirene ("bay of sirens") on the Punta San Vigilio.

A beach straight out of a travel magazine covers the northern part of the peninsula. It sits on private land, but a modest entrance fee opens the door to a truly unforgettable beach day under the cultivated olive groves on the lake.

The grounds protrude out into a bay and are surrounded by tree-covered hills from which the cypresses reach high into the sky. Relaxing in a lounge chair, you can work on your tan and enjoy the spectacular view, or take a dip in the crystal-clear waters and swim out to one of the two small swim platforms nearby. Refreshments are served at the bar and *gelateria*, and there is a children's play area, restrooms, and showers on-site.

The grounds are expansive, so you'll have no trouble staking out your own private spot under one of the olive trees. In this idyllic setting, you can find the peace and quiet that can be so easily lost amid the hurly-burly pace of the area during the tourist-filled summer months.

This sense of calm can be shaken up suddenly at any moment, however. The Lake Garda region is subjected to the elements from time to time with strong thunderstorms, as evidenced by the uprooted trunk of a tree among the row of cypresses just inside the gates to the Baia delle Sirene. This 300-year-old tree with its extraordinary length of nearly 100 feet and an estimated weight of ten tons was wrenched from the earth during a storm on the night of August 6, 1995.

Address Località San Vigilio, 37016 Garda (VR), Tel Parco Baia delle Sirene 0039/045/7255884, www.punta-sanvigilio.it | **Getting there** Punta San Vigilio and the Parco Baia delle Sirene are both accessible from the SR 249. | **Hours** Season begins in early May (weather permitting), Sat and Sun from 10am–6pm; June–Aug, 9:30am–8pm, Sun 9am–8pm; Sep, 10am–7pm (cashiers close 2 hours prior) | **Tip** On the SR 249 shortly before Torri del Benaco lies the small church of San Faustino, with beautiful frescoes dating from the 15th century.

14 Benacus, or Lake Garda

How Garda got its name

The Romans referred to this beautiful lake, known for its cliffs and promontories, as Benacus. Beginning in the early Middle Ages, however, that name would gradually be replaced by Lago di Garda. The name Benacus, though, has remained present in the minds of Italians. Dante speaks of "Benaco" in his early-14th-century masterpiece, *The Divine Comedy*. Even today, restaurants, hotels, and towns all over the region, such as San Felice del Benaco, keep the original appellation alive.

A myth explains the name change: the water god Benacus left the sea one day to climb Monte Baldo and ask the beautiful mountain nymph Engadina to be his companion. Though the pair loved each other deeply, Engadina missed her small mountain lake. In order to make her happy, Benacus promised her a much larger body of water. He struck his trident upon a rock, whereupon huge floods poured into a valley and converged to form a great lake. Engadina was overjoyed as she dove into the water and colored the lake with her beautiful blue hair. She soon gave birth to a son, whom Benacus named Garda – a name that would thereafter be given to the lake so beloved by his mother.

Visitors to the lake must see it in its geographic entirety: Garda is the largest lake in Italy, starting narrowly in the mountains of the north, extending over 32 miles in length, and gradually expanding into a large basin in the south. It is situated more than 200 feet above sea level and reaches a depth of up to 1135 feet. What has enchanted visitors from colder environs, from the barbarians to today's tourists, is the Mediterranean climate of the lake created by its unique topography. The high Alpine foothills protect the area from northerly winds, while the warmth from the Mediterranean Sea is carried in through the Po River Valley. This gives Garda's shores their more tropical fauna: palms, oleander, and trees bursting with olives and lemons.

Getting there The lake can be reached via the Strada Statale (SS) or Strada Regionale (SR). These roads are well signed, so navigation devices shouldn't be necessary. On the western shore, the Gardesana Occidentale (SS 45) leads from Riva to Salò, while on the eastern shore the Gardesana Orientale (SR 249) runs from Riva to Peschiera. You can reach Peschiera from Salò by taking the SS 572 from Salò to Desenzano and then the SS 11 from Desenzano to Peschiera. | **Tip** Lago di Ledro, about a 20-minute drive from Riva, is a very traditional small mountain lake and makes for a great day trip.

15_ The Friday Mercato
From underwear to grilled chicken

On market days, traffic into Garda backs up all the way to the high-way as everyone crowds into town, including both the locals looking to get their weekly shopping done as well as tourists in search of an adventure or a unique souvenir. Markets like the one in Garda take place on various days in different towns all around the lake. You can find just about anything under the sun, making the markets an important asset for the smaller towns often lacking in specialty stores.

During the week, many markets around Italy are dominated by quotidian mainstays like food and flower stalls. Perhaps thanks to the warm influence from the south of the country, there are usually just a handful of clothing vendors, but the markets around Lake Garda are exactly the opposite. Italians come here to buy their clothes and unmentionables, along with leather goods and trendy jewelry. This is what makes them so interesting to tourists. Not only can you pick up a beach towel for your day on the water but also a replacement for the belt you accidentally left at airport security. Many people pick up a souvenir from a household goods vendor, which for a native would just be a normal everyday appliance, such as a parmesan cheese grater, crumb sweeper (beautifully referred to in Italian as a *raccoglibriciole*), or a coffeepot to make an authentic Italian brew at home.

The Garda *mercato*, which always takes place on Fridays, is one of the largest in the area, its size varying based on the number of stalls that are set up on a given week. Vendors arrive early in the morning with their folding transporters or unloading their wares and filling their stalls directly from the trunks of their cars, and business runs all morning until 1pm.

The crowded market has been organized along the northern and southern ends of the lakefront, leaving the middle portion of the promenade free for the normal outdoor restaurant and café seating.

Address Mainly along the Lungolago Regina Adelaide, 37016 Garda (VR) | **Getting there** Take SR 249; street parking can be found across from the lakeshore or in one of the large parking lots nearby. | **Hours** Fridays, early morning – 1pm | **Tip** The long property of the Villa Albertini lies above the shore road; don't miss the beautiful view of the area from its obelisk-adorned gates.

16__ Palazzo del Capitano
A vestige of the town's historic past

The town of Garda has a beautiful wide promenade, the Lungolago, along the lake, and in its old town center there are many picturesque sights. Sometimes these can be a bit hard to find though, because Garda is undoubtedly one of the most touristy spots on the lake. When the locals grow weary of visitors – many of whom are from Germany – and refer to their lake as the *Lago dei Tedeschi* ("lake of the Germans"), they probably have Garda in mind.

Along the Lungolago, there are thousands of chairs set up for tourists to enjoy the view. While many are tempted to just sit and spend their entire visit admiring the shimmering lake, there are a handful of historic buildings around town that are worth looking at in more detail.

The Palazzo del Capitano stands among a row of buildings facing the lake and has a rather small footprint. The military superintendent, known as the Capitano del Lago, resided here intermittently while this area was under Venetian rule. The structure, built in the 14th and 15th centuries, embodies the period, with its Gothic-Venetian framed windows distributed irregularly over the facade. A few steps beyond lies the Lòsa, a building with a portico on the ground floor topped by a balcony. It was once part of a larger villa and combines a boathouse with a viewing platform.

The Calle dei Sottoportici, an alley spanned by brick arches, leads to the center of the mazelike town. As you travel from the Lungolago, the campanile stands on your right, while the Corso Vittorio Emanuele spurs off from the Palazzo Fregoso. This Renaissance palace, dating from the beginning of the 16th century, was built directly on top of the western gate to the city.

As you approach, keep your gaze cast upward in order to avoid the temptation to enter one of the narrow rooms that face the streets and are overflowing with clothing racks, reminiscent of an old oriental bazaar.

Address Lungolago Regina Adelaide / Piazza Catullo, 37016 Garda (VR) | **Getting there** From the SR 249, park directly along the lakeshore or in one of the large parking lots in town. | **Tip** Il Giardinetto, a restaurant located at Lungolago Regina Adelaide 27, is a good choice, specializing in dishes featuring lake and sea fish.

17__Punta San Vigilio

Refreshments at the prettiest spot on the lake

Sitting along the harbor at Punta San Vigilio on a sunny day, you'd be forgiven for pinching yourself to make sure that the incredibly beautiful view from the promontory looking out onto the lake was real. In the 16th century, Agostino Brenzoni purchased the site and had a large but tastefully restrained villa built here on the tip, or *punta*.

Today, the entire peninsula, including the villa, is privately owned by the Conti Guarienti di Brenzone. From the parking lot above the shore, a path lined by tall cypress trees leads you to the villa, nestled in a geometrically designed Renaissance garden *all'italiana*. To the left, the footpath continues down to the lake, and will guide you through an old alley past the historic property's outbuildings to the Locanda San Vigilio. From the beginning, this building served as an inn, and its rooms with their old wooden floors and lakeside loggias retain their original charm. Many prominent visitors are immortalized in the hotel guestbook, including Czar Alexander, Winston Churchill, Vivian Leigh, and Prince Charles. Today, the fine hotel and restaurant is run by Adriano Girardi.

Through an archway you'll enter the small harbor, the *porticciolo*, framed by a semicircle of old two-story buildings covered with sand-colored plaster. To one side is the Locanda, and to the other is the similarly designed Taverna building. Under its vine-covered pergola you can have a snack or sip a cappuccino, and the cafe is also a popular destination for private boats that dock at the harbor on day trips.

From the lake or from the outer end of the breakwater, you can see the chapel dedicated to the monk San Vigilio, who once lived here. Dating back to the 11th century, it is the oldest building in the entire complex.

On the north side of the peninsula lies Baia delle Sirene (see page 34) – perhaps Lake Garda's prettiest beach.

Address Località San Vigilio, 37016 Garda (VR), Tel. Hotel/Locanda
0039/045/7256688, Taverna 0039/045/7255190, www.punta-sanvigilio.it | **Getting
there** Lies along the SR 249; follow signs to the parking area. | **Hours** Mar–Oct,
Mon–Sun, the bar in the Taverna serves continuously from morning to evening | **Tip**
At the end of the cypress-lined path, an olive tree estimated to be more than
1000 years old stands to the left.

18 Rocca di Garda

A hike with spectacular views

If you're looking to squeeze in a workout while on vacation, a hike up the Rocca di Garda is a good option. The landscape of Garda is dominated by the imposing sight of the nearly 1,000-foot-tall mountain, officially named Monte Sairo. At its summit, the Lombards built a fortress, or *rocca* in Italian, which gave the mountain its nickname.

Trails up to the Rocca start at the church of Santa Maria Assunta at the southern end of town. From the parking lot to the left of the church, there is a gradually rising paved path, or a steeper, shorter trail with many steps to the right of the church. Sturdy shoes and a bottle of water are recommended in either case.

When asked how long the climb takes, Italians will usually reply with the same answer: *dipende come si cammina* ("it depends on how you walk"). You can expect the first part of the hike through the wild southern forest to take about three quarters of an hour, plus the final portion of the trail over the bare rock face. At the top of the mountain, the path winds past caves left over from archaeological excavations of the fortress. Today there is a wide-open platform at the end of the trail with simple wooden railings around its outer edges to prevent hikers from accidentally falling off the near-vertical cliff while posing for photos in front of the panoramic vista.

Wandering around at the top, a wide-angle view out over the entire expanse of Lake Garda opens before you, from Sirmione at the southern tip over the western shore to the mountains in the north. The bay directly below makes for an impressive sight, too, with the buildings of Garda and the headland of Punta San Vigilio marking its boundaries.

For Italians, climbing up Garda's local peak is a must. It is customary on holidays such as Easter to have a picnic atop the viewing platform, and if you venture up there at one of these times, you'll encounter mostly locals rather than tourists.

Address Santa Maria Assunta, Corso Italia 10, 37016 Garda (VR) | **Getting there** Take the SR 249 from Garda to the Baroque parish church. You can either park there or continue along Via Caboto to a larger parking lot. | **Tip** On your descent, you can make a detour to the monastery and church of the Camaldolese monks.

19_ The Heller Garden

A poetic interplay of plants and sculpture

"We hope that this unusual place will leave you all with happy hearts," writes Austrian multimedia artist André Heller in the brochure for his gardens. The roughly 2.5-acre botanical garden on the grounds of the Heller estate was originally laid out between 1910 and 1971 by the doctor and naturalist Arthur Hruska, who brought in over 2,000 plants representing all seven continents. These flora were interspersed with rocks, lakes, waterfalls, ponds and a babbling brook, and traversed by winding walking paths. In 1988, Heller purchased the gardens and enriched them with works of art by numerous artists, such as Mimmo Paladino, Roy Lichtenstein and Keith Haring.

At your first glimpse of the outer gate, designed by Heller with the symbol of the labyrinth, you'll already get a sense of the nature of his gardens. Though you'll receive a map upon entry, you'll be inclined to stow it away in your pocket and indulge all five senses fully in the experience.

The pathways are paved with various materials and textures. As you walk, a multitude of layered impressions unfolds, and new perspectives constantly take form. The air is thick with the fragrance of the plants, with a refreshing coolness, and with the chirping of countless birds.

Heller so succeeded in his desire to reflect the entire world in his garden that, with all of its international art and cultural objects, an almost supernatural aura exists. A bridge decorated with a statue of the Buddha fords a lily pond. Rounding a corner, a huge head appears with its eyes flashing, sporting an Indian mask decorated with colorful gems and stones, smoke swirling out of its huge mouth. The path through the bamboo forest is heavy with a haze produced by two monster heads spouting fine jets of water. The *Mostri Spuntanti*, a work produced by Heller himself, are the perfect embodiment of the dream world Heller takes joy in creating.

Address Giardino Botanico Fondazione André Heller, Via Roma 2, 25083 Gardone Riviera (BS), Tel 0039/0365/520247, www.hellergarden.com | **Getting there** Follow signs to the garden from state route (Strada Statale – SS) 45. | **Hours** Mar–Oct, Mon–Sun 9am–7pm | **Tip** Be sure to visit the cactus greenhouse at the most northerly end of the gardens for a game of chess or nine–men's morris.

20__ Torre San Marco

A tower above the rest

The spectacular Villa Alba draws everyone's attention like a magnet. Consequently, few people notice the beautiful tower across the road at all, especially since you can only grab a quick glimpse of its peak through the dense foliage of nearby trees.

The Villa Alba's owner Richard Langensiepen was by no means content with his splendid summer estate (see page 50), so he also built a small private harbor, where he parked his steam-powered motorboat – the first ever on Lake Garda. To top it all off, he erected an observation tower, called the Torre Ruhland, overlooking the harbor.

If his villa across the road took its design straight out of a pattern book of the architecture of ancient temples, a medieval castle fortress was apparently the model for the observation tower. Over a square foundation, the tower's stone masonry walls rise defiantly into the air. With its tiered roof structure, it is a sight to behold from the water.

It is quite amazing that throughout the tower's history (it was finished in 1902), it has attracted owners seeking the prestige of acquiring such a status symbol. Thus, Gabriele d'Annunzio purchased the tower in 1925 as a supplement to his nearby residence and renamed it the Torre San Marco. In the harbor, he moored the wooden torpedo boat MAS 96, which made him a hero of the First World War, though today it lies in its own separate building on the grounds of the Vittoriale (see page 52).

Starting in November 1943, Benito Mussolini began using the tower for romantic trysts with his mistress, Claretta Petacci, who lived in the neighboring Villa Fiordaliso.

Today the tower holds true to its intended tradition as a magnificent spot to host an event. During the summer months, the tower is beautifully lit and a piano bar and restaurant are open, with a DJ spinning on special nights. Otherwise the tower can be rented for private parties.

Address La Torre San Marco, Corso Zanardelli 132, 25083 Gardone Riviera (BS),
Tel 0039 / 0365 / 20158, www.torresanmarco.it | **Getting there** On the SS 45 directly
across from the Villa Alba, where you can also park. | **Hours** Call for current hours |
Tip In the building now housing the Ristorante Casinò at Corso Zanardelli 166, a
gaming casino was run from 1911 to 1912 and again at the beginning of the 1920s,
where it is said that King Farouk of Egypt lost a fortune.

21__ Villa Alba

A Greek-inspired mansion

A wide staircase staggered with multiple fountains runs high up to the Villa Alba, which looks like a copy of an ancient temple, with its statue-adorned portico resting atop powerful columns. The German businessman Richard Langensiepen from Magdeburg had this building constructed at the turn of the 20th century as his summer residence. In what certainly couldn't be called modesty, he is said to have guided his architect, Schaefer, to model his design after the monuments of the Acropolis in Athens.

While the Italian villas around the lake typically carry the family names of their owners, this impressive neoclassic-style building was called Alba by Langensiepen. The melodious feminine first name, which means "sunrise" in Italian, corresponds to the villa's location. It is facing east toward Lake Garda, and so receives the first rays of sunshine in the early-morning hours.

The German physician Ludwig Rohden praised the pleasant healthy climate of the area near Gardone Riviera in the publication *Deutschen Medizinischen Wochenzeitschrift* (German Medical Weekly) in October 1885. It soon after became a popular resort town and visitors began flocking here in large numbers to both cure their respiratory illnesses and to relax and unwind on vacation. This is probably the reason that led to the construction of the Villa Alba on this site.

Langensiepen was not able to enjoy his villa for very long, however, as the government took possession of the estate during World War I. Later, the villa served as the intelligence center of the Republic of Salò, then as the headquarters of one of Berlusconi's military undertakings.

In the 1970s, the Comune di Garda acquired the classical building for use as the first conference center on Lake Garda. Today, the Villa Alba is used for various cultural events, concerts and exhibitions.

Address Corso Zanardelli 73, 25083 Gardone Riviera (BS), www.villaalbaeventi.it |
Getting there The Villa Alba is on the SS 45 in the northern end of Gardone; there is a
parking lot to the right of the entrance. | **Hours** Not open to the public; the building is
only open for special events | **Tip** The Grand Hotel Gardone Riviera, founded in 1884,
is the oldest luxury hotel in the region, rebuilt in its current form in 1904.

22__Vittoriale degli Italiani
The shrine of Italian victories (and d'Annunzio)

Gabriele d'Annunzio seems to have been guided throughout his entire life by a single goal, namely to create an immortal mythos to his own persona. A visit to the Vittoriale degli Italiani lays this impression out before your eyes. In reality, this is not a monument to the victories of the Italians, as its name suggests, but rather a monument to the man who had it built.

D'Annunzio, the eccentric writer, womanizer, and hero of the First World War, is lauded as one of Italy's greatest writers, but is also a divisive figure because of his fascist political views and hedonistic lifestyle. He acquired the simple Villa Carnacco with its garden overlooking Lake Garda in 1921. He expanded it in the following years, converting it into an extravagant complex with the help of architect Giancarlo Maroni. In 1923, he renamed it Vittoriale and gifted the site to the Italian state, though he would continue to live there until his death in 1938.

The succession of dark, crowded rooms in the villa is a cross between a curiosity cabinet and a museum. Each room is assigned a function via an aphorism and staged with a smorgasbord of objects relating to the theme.

Particularly impressive is the Relic Room, in which sacred religious objects from many eastern and western traditions are gathered together with d'Annunzio's own personal holy objects, such as the dented wheel of a motorboat on which one of his close friends died during a particularly fast ride.

A walk through the approximately 22 acres of the grounds leads to the amphitheater or past the huge battleship *Puglia*, which looks as though it has run aground, culminating in the mausoleum, finished posthumously but according to d'Annunzio's specifications. In contrast to the *horror vacui* that reigns in the villa, the stark white marble sarcophagus of d'Annunzio rises from a ring of the ten memorial stones of his closest friends.

Address Via Vittoriale 12, 25083 Gardone Riviera (BS), Tel 0039/0365/296511,
www.vittoriale.it | Getting there Follow signs for the Vittoriale degli Italiani from the
SS 45. | Hours Mon–Sun 9am–5pm; tours are only available in Italian, but information
is available in other languages. | Tip The old district known as Gardone di Sopra, with
its ancient town center, invites visitors to linger among its many quaint restaurants.

23 __ Balls in the Walls
Recalling the high price of freedom

When you look at the facades of the historic houses that frame the picturesque harbor of Gargnano, you get the impression that a contemporary artist has recently completed some sort of public art project. Iron balls are lodged in the fronts of the buildings in loose succession – sometimes more, sometimes less, pushed deeply into the colorfully plastered masonry. Around the balls stretch iron bands.

While today these seem artistic and playful, they bear witness to an historical event that caused a wave of fear and terror to spread over the town. In 1866, during the fighting of the *Risorgimento*, as the Italian unification movement is known, Italian and French battleships withdrew to the harbor of Gargnano. The Austrians, who had ruled over much of northern Italy since the 1815 Congress of Vienna, launched an attack from Lake Garda with a squadron of six gunboats, and over several days Gargnano came under violent bombardment.

The former Palazzo del Municipio, the municipal building on the northern edge of the harbor, was also the target of shelling: one cannonball hit the outer corner of the building, the other smashed into the red plaster of the facade along the water. Under the loggia, the bombardment is commemorated with a marble plaque, with the specific dates of the attack listed: namely July 2, 4, 6, 19, and 20, 1866.

Since then, most of the houses standing around the Piazza Feltrinelli have been renovated. Regardless, the cannonballs were left exactly where they hit as a sign of Italy's painfully won independence, and the unification of the peninsula that was completed later that year.

Only Trentino, at the far northern tip of Lake Garda, remained under Habsburg rule, and was united with the rest of the Italian state at the end of World War I in 1919 after the defeat of the Austro-Hungarian Empire.

Address Palazzo del Municipio, Piazza Feltrinelli 3, 25084 Gargnano (BS) | **Getting there** Park in the underground garage at the intersection of the SS 45 and the one-way street leading to Centro. It is then about a 5-minute walk along the main street down to the harbor. | **Tip** The waterfront is dotted with orange trees, whose flowers give off a wonderful perfume in the summer.

24__Cloister of St. Francis

Columns that tell a tale

The church of San Francesco, built in 1280, is located at the southern end of Gargnano. The building's original appearance can still be seen in the red and white marble blocks of various sizes used to build the outer walls. The doorjambs at the western entrance are decorated with intricate flower buds.

The interior of the church was so heavily redone in later periods, however – especially the Baroque – that it might seem a disappointment. This letdown quickly fades, however, after you pass through the old coffered wooden gate to the right of the western facade of the building.

There you'll discover the cloister of the former monastery. Between the columns, which line the cross-vaulted passages to the open courtyard, are arches shaped like sweeping curtains. Each of the cube-shaped capitals of the columns is designed slightly differently. The citrus fruits and their respective foliage that are so typical of this region are depicted almost too realistically. You can also see pumpkins with their curling vines and various flowers, as well as fish, birds, and lions' heads. There is one capital showing human heads, arguably those of the Franciscan monks themselves. There are six columns on each side of the roughly 65-foot-long walkway. In the center of the courtyard, where originally a fountain was meant to stand, rises a tall cypress tree, the perfect culmination to the picturesque ensemble.

According to tradition, lemons were first introduced to the Lake Garda region by Franciscan monks, perhaps even by Saint Francis himself, who is said to have spent time in the monastery on the Isola del Garda in 1220.

In 1266, Saint Bonaventure founded the Franciscan monastery in Gargnano. It is therefore quite possible that the very first garden in the area in which citrus trees were cultivated was right here in the cloister.

Address Piazzale Boldini, 25084 Gargnano (BS) | **Getting there** From the SS 45, turn onto the one-way street toward Centro. | **Hours** Mon – Sun, from morning until evening | **Tip** Traveling further along the road, you will come upon a short stretch of lovely shops typical to Italian towns like this, ranging from those selling specialty foods and household goods to a *profumeria* and a *tabacchi*.

25__Limonaia Malora

Remembering the way things used to be

One of the few original *limonaie* (lemon greenhouses) remaining on the Lemon Riviera is the Limonaia Malora. The waterwheel and Malora stream running through the property contribute to its historic atmosphere. Giuseppe Gandossi has dedicated himself to this facility with great idealism. Its three tiers stagger up a steep slope, lined with tall coarse limestone pillars upon which old wooden beams rest. The trees, the oldest of which date back nearly a century, stand and thrive on these tiered platforms. Gandossi has calculated harvesting around 1,500 lemons alone from one of the oldest trees on the property.

Today it is a labor of love. The economic importance of lemons, for which the area was once so famous, is long gone. Cheap transport and the more simply managed cultivation of lemons in Sicily and in countries even farther south brought the industry to a halt in the early 20th century. In 1850, it had already suffered a sharp decline due to *gommosi* (brown-rot gummosis), a fungal infection, and most of the plants in the area were affected.

It will absolutely amaze you to see what measures are taken to protect the lemons during the cool winter months. Frames with glass panels are assembled on the tiers, and boards are laid across the beams. Small clay pots filled with water are fixed to the lemon trees, which act as a frost-warning system. Should there be a thin layer of ice atop the water, the air is heated immediately by means of small hearths.

Aside from the sales of limoncello, a profitable side business of the Limonaia Malora is found in the caper bushes, with their wonderfully beautiful flowers, that grow along the back walls. The capers are processed on-site and are a typical delicacy of Gargnano, used to liven up the local fish dishes. The lizards climbing here and there in the gardens assist with the distribution of seeds, just as they would in the wild.

Address Giuseppe Gandossi, Via della Libertà 2, 25084 Gargnano (BS),
Tel 0039/0365/71840 | Getting there Located at the southern end of town right on
the SS 45. | Hours By appointment only at the Proloco Gargnano (Ufficio turistico),
reached at Tel 0039/0365/72082; visits held each Friday starting at 10am; for
information you can also contact Gianfranco Scanferlato, Hotel Garni Riviera,
(Via Roma 1, 25084 Gargnano) | Tip A historic oven in which the residents of
Gargnano once baked their bread can be seen through the window of the small
exhibition space in Via Forni 20; the artist Mariano Fuga shows his sculptures here.

26__La Tortuga
A highly acclaimed family-run restaurant

A visit to La Tortuga alone makes a trip to Lake Garda worthwhile. The restaurant, which sits near the small harbor of Gargnano, has no external signs, but everyone will know the room, with its old, wood-beamed ceiling. The grandmother of the current manager, Orietta Filippini, ran a rustic *osteria* on the site until it was converted into a full-service restaurant in the 1960s by her parents, Danilo and Maria Filippini, and since 1980 it has continuously kept its Michelin star rating.

A pleasant intimacy reigns in the small room decorated in deep reds, because only about 20 people can be accommodated at a time. Guests are treated with the great charm and professional matter-of-course typical of a traditional family business. Besides Orietta, her father still works as a sommelier and provides excellent recommendations from the wine list, which includes some 800 selections.

Orietta's mother, Maria Filippini, remains in the kitchen working as the chef, and her dishes, or *piatti*, are so well prepared that after each course you're tempted to run back and throw your arms around her. Initially, it is a treat for the eyes to see before you the fine china with its composition, decorated with flowers; but at first bite, you realize just what your taste buds are actually capable of.

The menu, which is described as "classic and innovative," includes fish both from Lake Garda and the ocean, as well as hearty meat dishes. Special emphasis is placed on fresh produce and high-quality local ingredients from the surrounding countryside, and because of this the menu changes seasonally and depending on market conditions.

There is undoubtedly an art to creating dishes so that the flavors of the individual ingredients really shine as the result of how they are combined.

The excellence of the food paired with the inviting environment makes for a dining experience that is true perfection.

Address Via XXIV Maggio 5, 25084 Gargnano (BS), Tel and Fax 0039/0365/71251, la.tortuga@alice.it | **Getting there** Park in the underground garage at the intersection of the SS 45 and the one-way road leading to Centro. It is then about a 5-minute walk along the main road to the left down to the harborfront. | **Hours** Wed–Mon from 7pm, closed Tuesdays; reservations recommended | **Tip** Be sure to take a look at the happily rocking figure at the entrance created by local artist Mariano Fuga. It depicts Orietta's credo: *Lavoro come divertimento!*

27 — Villa Feltrinelli

A grand hotel in a family of entrepreneurs' summer home

The Villa Feltrinelli continues to follow in the spirit of its original owners, the entrepreneurial Feltrinelli family. In 1892, the Feltrinellis built a sprawling summer home designed by the Milanese architect Alberico Barbiano di Belgioioso along the shores of Lake Garda, including vast grounds and manicured gardens. Today, the villa operates as an exclusive hotel, where guests who stay for the warmer months of the year continue in the grand tradition of this luxurious retreat.

It must have taken substantial effort and talent to restore the former glory of this handsome neo-Gothic style building, whose original interior and opulent furnishings sat dusty and disused for many years. The park, with its many old trees, was recreated, and the outbuildings, such as the boathouse and *limonaia* (lemon greenhouse), were refurbished. The villa has been aesthetically and functionally updated with today's modern amenities and conveniences. The reconstruction lasted about five years after Bob H. Burns, founder of the Regent International Hotels, acquired this beautiful gem. Since 2001, the Villa Feltrinelli has been run by hotelier Markus Odermatt.

The villa has also seen its share of history. From 1943 to 1945, the Nazis quartered Benito Mussolini here under the watchful eye of the SS. Winston Churchill is rumored to have visited Il Duce on a secret mission to offer safe exile, but as we know, his mission was unsuccessful. When Mussolini later fled to nearby Lake Como, he was shot by partisans, along with his mistress, Claretta Petacci.

Today there is a spur off the main road from Gargnano that leads directly to the gates of the hotel, which visitors will initially find closed and must ring a bell for admittance.

One need not be a registered overnight guest to enjoy a relaxing aperitif on the terrace or visit the Michelin-starred restaurant located inside.

Address Grand Hotel a Villa Feltrinelli, Via Rimembranza 38–40, 25084 Gargnano (BS), Tel 0039/0365/798000, www.villafeltrinelli.com | **Getting there** Take the SS 45 to the Centro spur and continue straight until you reach the hotel gates. | **Tip** Continuing on the road parallel to the lakeshore will take you to the small Romanesque church of San Giacomo di Calino, which has frescoes dating from the 15th century.

28__The Lemons of Limone
Nomen est omen

If you were to ask people on the street what they think of when they hear about the town of Limone on Lake Garda, they would probably look at you a bit askance and reply, "Well, lemons of course": *limone* means "lemons" in Italian! In reality, however, the name of the town has nothing to do with citrus, but rather comes from the Latin word *limes*, which means "boundary." Until the end of World War I, the border between Italy and Austria ran right through here.

The steep mountain slopes surrounding the town have supported groves of lemon trees for several hundred years, but it was a group of enterprising locals who first made the lemon their trademark. It helped boost tourism in the town during the *Wirtschaftswunder*, or the economic miracle years of the 1950s, when loads of Germans proudly drove over the Alps in their newly affordable cars. Thus the sleepy fishing village at the foot of the imposing Dosso dei Roveri mountains evolved into a popular tourist destination. Not all of the changes that occurred in Limone were for the better, however, as the increase in tourism brought with it huge crowds and often large, unappealingly designed hotels.

Today, Limone is one of the most populated places on Lake Garda. The bars, restaurants, and shops along the wide waterfront promenade ply their offerings directly to the tourists. You can find anything and everything having to do with lemons in the shops here: from limoncello and olive oil with lemon juice to candied citrus fruits and various ceramic wares decorated with lemons.

You may be able to find that perfect memento of your time here to bring home with you, but keep in mind that the souvenirs sold in Limone are probably not manufactured in town. The lemons used in the products are likely imported from Sicily, and the beautiful white bowls decorated with yellow lemons are manufactured in Bassano del Grappa.

Address Via Lungolago Marconi, 25010 Limone sul Garda (BS) | **Getting there** From the SS 45, follow signs towards Centro; there is a large parking lot in front of the harbor. | **Tip** Delicious dried citrus fruits can be found in the small shop Mirella Delikatessen at Via Lungolago Marconi 14.

29_Pietra di Castelletto
Mysterious messages from the Bronze Age

The first stone slab covered in enigmatic characters was discovered in the mid-1960s at Castelletto by the scholar Mario Pasotti. The Pietra di Castelletto captured everyone's attention, and more petroglyphs were gradually uncovered in the area between Malcesine and Garda. To date, more than 250 stones with some 3,000 representations are known, probably dating from the Bronze Age in the 2nd millennium B.C. All of the characters were carved using the same technique. The rocks, polished smooth during the Ice Age, served as the "canvas." Small pointed depressions were then chiseled into the slabs using a type of hammer, and were connected into lines. Their light color stands out from the darker hues of the stone.

If you drive down to Magugnano on the lakeshore, you'll find the *municipio*, or municipal building, for the city of Brenzone. The Pietra di Castelletto is now on display in its foyer. On close inspection, marks are visible on the approximately 13-by-5.5-foot stone slab, though they are hardly decipherable.

A small-scale drawing of the markings is clearer and easier to understand, and draws your attention to two areas of images. In the first one, axes and daggers are shown, while in the other there is a labyrinth with seven axes. It is believed that the figurations had a religious significance. Perhaps the stone also marked a trade route between the Alps region and the Po Valley.

Other petroglyphs that have been discovered show depictions of human figures, some of them on horses, along with animals and religious symbols.

It is now widely believed that the artists responsible for creating the pictures were the hunters and shepherds who populated the area at that time, or even those who were searching for quartz-bearing rocks or metals such as limonite. But it remains a mystery, or better left to our imagination, what exactly they were trying to communicate.

Address Municipio, Comune di Brenzone, Via XX Settembre 8, 37010 Magugnano di Brenzone (VR), Tel 0039/045/6589500 | **Getting there** From the SR 249 head toward Magugnano; there is a parking lot at the Municipio. | **Hours** The lobby is open Mon–Thurs 9am–1pm and 3–6pm, Fri 9am–1pm | **Tip** From the Municipio, it is worth taking a stroll through the very unique town of Magugnano, with its small harbor.

30__Funivia Monte Baldo

A panoramic ride up to great heights

There is no better way to spend a nice, clear day while visiting the region than a trip up Monte Baldo. With the *funivia*, or cable car, you travel from 300 to 5,775 feet above sea level in a matter of minutes. The ride in itself is already sensational, because the round gondola car is encircled by a ribbon of windows and rotates as you ascend. The first views of Malcesine expand into a breathtaking panoramic perspective of the entirety of Lake Garda, including the mountains on the opposite shore.

The mountain massif of Monte Baldo stretches for nearly 22 miles along the eastern shore of Lake Garda and reaches heights of over 6,500 feet. Various routes are signposted at the mountain station, so you can opt for a hike depending on your physical condition and level of desire. In addition to a reading trail that provides information about flora and fauna, there are also guided tours offered from late May to September. During the last Ice Age, the mountain was surrounded by glaciers, but not covered. Therefore, an almost unique pre-Ice Age vegetation was preserved on its high plateau. In addition to the various orchids, edelweiss, and gentian, a wild peony known as the Monte Baldo sedge blooms in the high Alpine meadows.

During the summer months, mountain bikers begin their adventurous descent of the trails and paragliders sail down to the lake from the mountain station. In the heart of winter, the same station is transformed into a high-altitude ski resort. As long as there is enough snow cover, there are five lifts open, along with the Baldo Snowpark.

Returning to the base station, you can view the small, old red-painted gondola that was in operation from 1962 until 2001. In July 2002, the new *funivia*, with its futuristic stations and spinning windowed cabins, was inaugurated by then president of the Italian Republic Carlo Azeglio Ciampi.

Address Via Navene Vecchia 12, 37018 Malcesine (VR), Tel. 0039 / 045 / 7400206, www.funiviedelbaldo.it | **Getting there** The base station lies directly along the SR 249; there is a garage available on site. | **Hours** The cable car runs every 30 minutes from end of Mar to mid-Sep, Mon–Sun 8am–6pm; mid-Sep to early Oct, Mon–Sun 8am–5pm; early Oct to early Nov, Mon–Sun 8am–4pm; call for winter hours | **Tip** There are a handful of dining options available on the top of Monte Baldo, such as the Bar Caffè Cime del Baldo at the funivia station.

31___Goethe's Bust

An homage to Germany's poet prince

The journal kept by Johann Wolfgang von Goethe, one of the most revered German writers, poets, and statesmen of all time, during his Italian travels in 1786 offers many observations of the conditions he found in the region. After he crossed the Brenner Pass, he must have quite spontaneously decided not to travel directly through the Val d'Adige on to Verona, writing, "This evening I could have seen Verona, but the natural scenery along the way was just so beautiful; a beautiful spectacle, this Lago di Garda."

His trip took him to Torbole, and since at that time there was no road built along the shore, he set off from there in the early morning hours of September 13 on a boat with two rowers heading south. They had to change their planned course, however, "when the wind completely reversed," and instead ended up at the harbor of Malcesine, the "first stop within the Venetian State," as Torbole at that time was in Austrian territory.

On that first boat trip, Goethe had already drawn his first sketch of the Scaligeri Castle in Malcesine (see page 74). After disembarking, he made additional drawings of the abandoned castle and was quickly surrounded by locals who approached him angrily, thinking that he was a spy for the Austrian emperor. The mayor was called, along with a certain Gregorius, who had previously worked with a family in Frankfurt, Germany. Common acquaintances and the urbane appearance of Goethe quickly diffused their suspicions, however, and they subsequently offered help and safe passage.

A *Sala di Goethe* (room dedicated to Goethe) has been set up to commemorate this event by the Scaligeri Castle in cooperation with the Casa di Goethe in Rome. In front of the museum, Goethe is immortalized in a bronze bust surrounded by blossoming impatiens. It depicts the exalted author with his very wide traveling hat, the same one we remember him wearing in the well-known portrait by Tischbein.

Address Castello Scaligero Malcesine, Via Castello 39, 37018 Malcesine (VR), Tel 0039/045/6570333 | **Getting there** Follow signs to the parking lot from the SR 249, or park in the garage at the Funivia Monte Baldo. | **Hours** Apr–Oct, Mon–Sun 9:30am–6:30pm; Nov–Mar, Sat and Sun 11:30am–4pm; because winter hours can change on short notice, calling ahead is recommended | **Tip** At a house below the castle, at Via Catullo 11, there is a plaque remembering that Goethe drew its arch.

32 Palazzo dei Capitani

A lakeside sanctuary

The imposing Palazzo dei Capitani is located on the Via Capitanato right along the harbor. Its entryway opens into a large hall, spanned by a wide, shallow barrel vault. On the ceiling, there is a fresco depicting the Lion of St. Mark dating from 1672.

In the 13th and 14th centuries, the palace served as the seat of the Scaligeri family. In December 1473, it passed into the ownership of the Miniscalchi family, who rebuilt it in its current form. Between 1405 and 1797, during the time that the eastern shore of Lake Garda was ruled by Venice, a *capitano*, or captain, was seated for military security and to oversee parts of the administration. He was headquartered alternately among Malcesine, Torri, and Garda. In 1618, the Republic of Venice acquired the palazzo and moved the residence of the *capitano* here from a building in the Scaligeri castle. In 1897, ownership was passed to Malcesine, and in 1902, the Palazzo dei Capitani was declared a national monument, and was opened to the public.

From the main hall, you walk through a wrought-iron gate out to the palm garden. With its lakefront setting surrounded by walls topped with battlements, the gravel courtyard with its flowerbeds and towering palm trees seems like an oasis. On benches or in the small on-site restaurant you can enjoy the idyllic location where the captain would have at one time entered directly from the dock after tying his boat off.

The facade of the palazzo facing the lake is arranged symmetrically: the windows on the upper floors are enclosed just as the entry way is by a fine stone framing in the style of the early Renaissance. The rounded arches atop the lateral pilasters clearly demonstrate that the palace was not rebuilt by the Venetians. They would most certainly have left their unique mark through the use of typical gothic-Venetian framing, such as that found at the Palazzo del Capitano in Garda (see page 40).

Address Via Capitanato 8, 37018 Malcesine (VR) | **Getting there** Follow signs to the parking lot from the SR 249, or park in the garage at the Funivia Monte Baldo. | **Hours** Generally open daily | **Tip** You will find the tourist office of Malcesine Più, next door at Via Capitanato 6, in which you can find information and buy tickets for current events and concerts.

33_ The Scaligerian Fort

Extreme sports in an extremely beautiful setting

The old rustic buildings of Malcesine, with their rough limestone masonry plastered in clay, offer a completely different picture from the colorful facades in the other towns along the lake. The castle overlooking the town stands proudly atop the edges of the rocky cliffs at the end of the gravel-paved Via Castello.

But to refer to this vast complex, with its three courtyards, numerous buildings, and spiral ramps leading up to the 230-foot-high central *mastio*, or fortified tower, as merely a castle or fortress seems almost an understatement.

Alberto della Scala commissioned the construction of this seat of power in 1277, incorporating the structures built by his predecessors on this spot, including a Lombard fort. The topography of the location on the rocks protruding into the lake offered an ideal defensive position for centuries.

The Palazzo Veneziano lies just behind the entrance to the castle, which until 1618 served as the office of the Venetian *capitano* (see page 72). From 1798 to 1866, the Austrians used it as a barracks, and today it houses a branch of the Natural History Museum. Its exhibits are dedicated to the theme of Lake Garda, and the suggestive panoramic projections presented in one of the rooms in the basement give the impression of being submerged in the lake teeming with fish.

The courtyard of this lower terrace extends up to a crenellated wall, which offers a breathtaking panoramic view. It is exactly from this outer wall, over the cliffs, which plunge steeply into the lake, that Red Bull has hosted its Cliff Diving World Series competitions over the last few years. From an attached springboard, the cliff divers jump in ornate formations down nearly 90 feet into the water.

The event has become increasingly popular, and is watched by many curious spectators along the shore and from their boats anchored nearby.

Address Via Castello 39, 37018 Malcesine (VR), Tel 0039/045/6570333 | **Getting there** Follow signs to the parking lot from the SR 249, or park in the garage at the Funivia Monte Baldo. | **Hours** Apr–Oct, Mon–Sun 9:30–6:30pm; Nov–Mar, Sat and Sun 11:30am–4pm; because winter hours can change on short notice, calling ahead is recommended. For details about the cliff diving competitions visit www.redbullcliffdiving.com or www.malcesinepiu.it. | **Tip** It is worth a trip into town to walk through its winding, labyrinthine alleys, some of which are so narrow that a person can barely fit through.

34__ The Mincio
The loveliest way out of Lake Garda

The lake has about twenty-five rivers flowing into it, the largest of which is the Sacra River in the north. There is only one flowing out, however: the Mincio, which emerges in Peschiera dell Garda at the southern tip of the lake. From here it flows through the picturesque moraine landscape to Mantua, where it continues toward the Adriatic Sea for about fifty miles, finally draining into the Po near Governolo.

In the 1950s, a flood-control dam was built across the Mincio south of Peschiera. Since then, the water level in the river has been regulated to prevent flooding during heavy rainfalls and to divert water for the irrigation of the agricultural areas during dry seasons. Therefore, the low water level of the lake in the warm summer months is not just caused by evaporation.

The pentagonal fortress town of Peschiera lies within the funnel through which the Mincio begins its path southward. The town is completely surrounded by water, and a channel runs through its center. The historic waterway is used today as a harbor, and colorful boats bob up and down in the deep blue water on both sides of the river.

The Mincio begins its journey through the five arches built into the powerful architecture of the fortress's brick masonry, a bastion of the time of Austrian rule. It is truly a sight to behold.

In his *Divine Comedy*, the famous Italian poet Dante Alighieri extolled the special situation in Peschiera, which remains much unchanged since he wrote his masterpiece at the beginning of the 14th century: "Sitteth Peschiera, fortress fair and strong … Where round about the bank descendeth lowest. There of necessity must fall whatever, In bosom of Benaco cannot stay, And grows a river down through verdant pastures. Soon as the water doth begin to run, No more Benaco is it called, but Mincio, Far as Governo, where it falls in Po.

Address 37019 Peschiera del Garda (VR) | **Getting there** From the SR249 to the roundabout in front of the old town, drive to a parking lot at the water's edge; the old fortified city is pedestrianized. | **Tip** There are many inviting restaurants along the canal, such as the very nice Pizzeria Al Canal, at Via Fontana 5.

35 __ Porta Verona

Instilling fear in the hearts of the enemy

The most important entrance into the old walled town of Peschiera is marked by the Porta Querina, also known as the Porta Verona because its outer walls are oriented toward the road leading to Verona. Pilasters frame the central arched passageway and the shorter lateral passages.

The proud expression of the gatehouse is also reflected in the engraving on the entablature near the roof. In large letters, the Latin inscription reads: *disce haec moneat praecelsa leonis imago ne stimules veneti cev leo in hoste vigent MDLIII.* The translation of the warning reads: "You should know that this extraordinary image of the lion is to prevent you from provoking the Venetians, because against their enemies they have the strength of a lion." The gate's year of construction (1553) is added at the end.

Where the fear-inducing symbol of the Venetian Republic once majestically stood, however, there is now only a bit of damaged masonry left to see. With a little effort and imagination, however, you can recognize the outline of the Lion of St. Mark, which had indeed provoked the occupying forces of the city much as its builders had intended.

The city at the southern tip of Lake Garda, strategically important since Roman times and often fought over, was expanded by the Republic of Venice from 1553 to 1556 into an imposing fortress city in the shape of a five-pointed star. The fortifications were again strengthened while under the occupation of Napoleon's French forces in the early 19th century, then once again under Austrian rule in 1815.

The southern area of the town is still dominated by military buildings. Some are used as they were originally intended, as Peschiera is now a location of the Italian army. Others have been converted into museums and some stand empty, such as the Austrian barracks extending along the central canal.

Address Via Venezia, 37019 Peschiera del Garda (VR) | **Getting there** Take the SR 249, which is called Via Venezia coming from the east, to the roundabout; the gate is located straight ahead; from the roundabout, drive to the waterfront for parking. | **Tip** Surrounded by the waters of the Mincio, the outer walls of the fortress offer a great location for a waterside walk.

36__ Riva Boats
An up-close look at luxury

More than 40 years ago, Cesare Casarola founded the company that has since held the exclusive right to sell the boats with the Riva brand in Italy. Today he runs it alongside his children Francesca, Monica, and Edoardo.

A Riva boat remains the unbeatable classic among luxury motorboats. The showroom of Nautica Casarola has several models of boats from different eras on display. These are all used, and many are there to be repaired or restored in the workshops of the 70,000-square-foot facility.

New boats are all built to order, and as a rule the lucky buyers pick up their new toys directly from the factory. This facility is located in nearby Sarnico on the small Lago d'Iseo.

Riva boats don't take their name from the town on the northern tip of Lake Garda, but rather from the first boat builder, Pietro Riva. The story is a legend in these parts. A fisherman from Sarnico was looking for someone who could fix his boats, which had been badly damaged in a storm. He met Pietro Riva by chance in Como in 1842, and Riva executed the needed repairs perfectly. His reputation spread, and Riva received further orders for repairs and for new boats. He founded the operation in Sarnico, which his sons continued to lead for three generations.

Under Carlo Riva, the company eventually developed into the industry leader in the 1950s, and in 1962 they released the Aquarama, a sporty and elegant boat with mahogany paneling, sweeping lines, and the potential to go up to 45 miles per hour – the epitome of a Riva boat.

The brand's boat-building tradition is continued today by its present owner, the Ferretti Group, but the Aquarama is no longer manufactured. The sight of the 26-foot-long example on display at Nautica Casarola still conjures up the company's classic advertising slogan: *sun, sea, joy of living!*

Address Nautica Casarola S.r.l., Via Marco Biagi 7, 37019 Peschiera del Garda (VR), Tel 0039/045/6401412, www.nauticacasarola.com | **Getting there** The showroom is located near the highway exit for Peschiera del Garda; from there take the SS 11 toward Sirmione/Brescia. After a third of a mile, turn left at Località Zanina, then right onto Via Marco Biagi. | **Tip** When you're done admiring the Riva boats, consider an excursion through the Mincio river valley to Valeggio sul Mincio, famous for its idyllic hillside covered by expansive vineyards.

37__Santuario del Frassino
The miraculous help of a small statuette

The pilgrimage church of Madonna del Frassino lies just outside the center of Peschiera on the spot where a miracle is believed to have occurred.

The story goes that in 1510, as a farmer named Bartolomeo Broglia worked in his field, he was threatened by a snake. He prayed to the Virgin Mary for help, who appeared in the form of a small statue bathed in light in an alder tree (in Italian called a *frassino*) and drove away the snake. The farmer took the statuette home, but the Madonna inexplicably returned to the alder tree unnoticed. The same thing was repeated several times, after which local church leaders locked the figure up in a tabernacle.

In 1518, Franciscan monks built a church and convent on this spot. They cared for the site for about three centuries, until they were expelled in 1810 by Napoleonic troops, who desecrated the buildings and repurposed them for civilian use. In 1898 the friars were called back to revive the ruined church, and to this day, the Franciscans look after the *santuario* and its visitors.

The small church, whose vestibule opens out into a wide square, has loggias running along both sides and is picturesquely framed by cypresses.

The Madonna statuette is seen in a tabernacle in the southern side of the chapel. The five-and-a-half-inch-tall terra-cotta sculpture of Mary holding the infant Jesus is placed in the hollow of a gnarled tree trunk, a brilliant crown atop her head. It is bathed in a mystical light, and seems like an apparition. Two angels hold another crown above her, which was given to the church by the Vatican in 1930. A snake slithers up the trunk from below.

Loud birdsong beckons from the adjacent cloister, which houses an aviary in the center. Another cloister follows, whose walls are covered with painted and embroidered pictures, tiles, photographs, and letters, all offering their thanks to the Madonna for her assistance.

Address Via Frassino 4, 37019 Peschiera del Garda (VR), www.santuariodelfrassino.it | **Getting there** Signs will guide you from anywhere in Peschiera. | **Hours** In summer, daily 6:30am–12pm and 3–7:30pm; in winter, daily 6:30am–12pm and 2:30–7:30pm | **Tip** The parking lot in front also serves the local cemetery, which extends behind the loggia on the right. A stop there is exemplary of Italian funereal culture.

38__Gardesana Occidentale

A road worth taking

People traveling down from the north over the Alps in earlier times would have had to get in a boat in order to continue their journey beyond Riva. About 12 miles south, they could again go ashore in Gargnano and travel on by road. But in 1931, a new highway called the Gardesana Occidentale was built along the steep rock faces that line the lake in this part of the region. This daring engineering feat is considered today to be one of the most spectacular scenic drives in all of Italy.

As you drive along the road between Riva and Gargnano, you'll pass through 74 tunnels and over more than 50 bridges. Drivers should certainly leave the counting to their passengers, however, since their concentration should remain squarely on the road. Driving through these tunnels requires some skill and patience. Some are very narrow, and you can only hope that there is no bus coming from the other direction; some are bored straight through the stone, others are lined with concrete. Many of the tunnels are not illuminated, and often the sunlight pouring in rhythmically through the lateral slits in the walls is as distracting as a strobe light. You'll exhale deeply as you emerge from these tunnels, when a broad curve in the road affords you a wide, calming view of the lake.

The Pra de la Fam *limonaia* (lemon greenhouse), lying right along the road in Tignale, offers travelers a well-earned breather. Its name, which means "hunger meadow," reminds today's visitors that this spot offered the fishermen of yesteryear the only place to land their boats when surprised by a storm. They would be marooned here and forced to wait until the sea calmed down again.

The *limonaia* was originally built in the middle of the 18th century on the small plateau below the rock massif. The greenhouse was later abandoned, but today, under the direction of an experienced gardener, new lemon trees have been planted and are once again fruit-bearing.

Getting there From Riva, the Gardesana Occidentale is marked as SS45 through Limone to Gargnano. | **Tip** The spectacular Cascata del Varone, a nearly 330-foot-high waterfall in the river Varone, is located about two miles north of Riva in the direction of Tenno.

39_Santa Maria Inviolata

A devotional image in the Baroque church

At the intersection of the main streets in Riva lies the church of Santa Maria Inviolata. The central building is adorned sparingly from the outside, but as you enter the church, the rich Baroque ornamentation unfolds, covering every square inch of surface.

A tabernacle sits atop the altar, decorated with a faded representation of the enthroned Madonna with the infant Jesus in her arms, flanked by Saints Roch and Sebastian. This image was the reason for building the church in the first place.

Originally the Zanardi family had donated the piece toward the end of the 16th century, and it adorned the outer wall of one of the altars, which was on the site of the Moses Fountain beside the church today. The image of Mary soon came to be regarded as miraculous. A small temporary wooden chapel was built to protect it, but it was soon bursting at the seams. Numerous donations were collected in regular Marian devotions, and the Prince-Bishop of Trient, Cardinal Carlo Madruzzo, along with wealthy families from the area provided funds for the construction of a new devotional church.

The church building and its adjoining cloisters were built according to the plans of a Portuguese architect brought in from Rome, whose name has been lost to the ages. When the fresco was transferred to the new altar in 1636, the church was consecrated. Just like the magnificent decoration of the central church building, the renaming of the parish from Madonna dello Spiazzo (Madonna of the Place) to Maria Inviolata (the Virgin Mary) stands firmly rooted in the Counter-Reformation.

The octagonal interior with its four concave vaulted chapels is divided by pilasters, which are so imaginatively decorated that they alone deserve an attentive look. Allow your gaze to wander high up to the elaborately frescoed ceiling of the dome, where Mary actually seems to be rising into heaven.

Address Largo Marconi, 38066 Riva del Garda (TN) | **Getting there** Located at the intersection of the Gardesana Occidentale with the roads from Arco and from Tenno and between Viale Trento and Viale Roma. There is a parking lot at the church. | **Hours** Mon–Sun 9am–5pm | **Tip** From the church, Viale Roma leads you to the old city gate, the Porta San Michele, and connects you further to the town center, which today is a pedestrian zone.

40 Torre Apponale

The angelic weathervane symbolizing the city

The Torre Apponale, the medieval town tower, rises alongside the central Piazza III Novembre at the old harbor of Riva. Its name is explained by its orientation toward the small village of Ponale, and its eponymous river in the southwest. The tower, first mentioned in writing in 1273, was built to control the transport of goods and as an early warning system for approaching threats. The city was fought over for centuries, and the watchtower was frequently put to good use.

The most important moment in the history of Riva was on November 3, 1918, the date that lends its name to the surrounding piazza. On that day, Italian troops landed in the harbor, effectively ending Austrian rule on Lake Garda.

The historic event was also the reason for a structural change to the tower made in the 1920s. An onion dome, which can still be seen in many old pictures of the tower, was eliminated, since it reminded people all too well of typical Austrian architecture. The new flat pyramidal roof replaced it and is crowned with a golden, trumpet-blowing angel, the Anzolim de la Tor, which has since become the symbol of Riva.

The tower, built of rough-hewn stone blocks, stands on a square footprint and rises with a slight taper to a height of more than 110 feet. The upper portion, with its coupled arched openings on all four sides, was only added in 1555. Since the most recent renovation in 2002, you can climb up a wooden staircase inside to this platform. As a reward for ascending the 165 steps to the top, you are presented with a magnificent view of Lake Garda, the city, and the mountains beyond.

There is documentation dating back to the middle of the 14th century that the Torre Apponale also functioned as a clock tower. The bronze bells of the town were cast in 1532, and today still chime every quarter hour between 7am and 9pm.

Address Piazza III Novembre, 38066 Riva del Garda (TN) | **Getting there** Park at the intersection of the Gardesana Occidentale with the roads from Arno and from Tenno; follow the pedestrian zone to the tower and its golden angel. | **Hours** June–Aug, Mon–Sun 10am–6pm; Mar–May and Sep–Oct, Tue–Sun 10am–6pm; closed Nov–Mar. | **Tip** There are several restaurants with outdoor terraces along the harbor.

41 Gasparo da Salò
A famous violin maker on the waterfront promenade

Salò is the only place on Lake Garda with a definite urban flair. The wide shoreline promenade is lined with stately palaces painted in warm, bright earth tones, housing elegant shops and inviting bars and restaurants. Countless boats bob up and down next to one another in the long, curved bay, the extent of which can only truly be appreciated from a bird's-eye view.

This captivating scenery arose as a result of a cataclysmic event. On October 30, 1901, an earthquake shook beneath the western shores of Lake Garda, and the wealthy old city of Salò was almost completely destroyed. On the ruins of the old town, the impressive new promenade was built, much wider, and pulled far out into the lake. At the same time, the palazzos and other buildings were reconstructed or renovated, fundamentally transforming the image of the city, a testament to the prosperity and large fund-raising efforts of its people.

The Lungolago, as the promenade is called, is named for Giuseppe Zanardelli, immortalized there in a bronze effigy. The jurist and statesman, who was actually from Brescia but often stayed in Salò, was the acting prime minister during the construction of the promenade, until 1903.

A second sculpture remembers another famous son of the city, namely Gasparo Bertolotti, also known as Gasparo da Salò, who lived from 1540 to 1609. The bust made of green patinated bronze stands between tall cypress trees, and depicts the musician and founder of a private violin-making school deeply absorbed in his work. The statue seems to perfectly illustrate the quote by the famous Italian writer and poet Gabriele d'Annunzio, which can be read on the pedestal: *non si sa se stia aprendo il petto per trarne il violino o se stia aprendo il violino per mettervi il cuore* ("You do not know if he is opening his chest to pull out a violin, or if he is opening the violin to place therein his heart").

Address Lungolago Zanardelli (above Vicolo San Giovanni), 25087 Salò (BS) | **Getting there** From the SS 45, drive in the direction of Salò Centro, and park before reaching the old city, as it is a pedestrian zone. | **Tip** If you continue northwest along the Lungolago, you'll reach the cathedral, which is well worth a visit.

GASPARO DA SALO'

INVENTORE DEL VIOLINO

1540 - 1609

42__ Republic of Salò
Mussolini's government in exile

Salò will unfortunately go down in history ingloriously as the capital of the *Repubblica Sociale Italiana* (RSI), or Italian Social Republic. During the closing stages of World War II, as the Allied troops made landfall in Sicily, the fascist government collapsed and Benito Mussolini was overthrown by his own people. Freed by German paratroopers, he was reinstated at the behest of his old ally Adolf Hitler, and was installed as the head of the puppet regime proclaimed in September 1943, often referred to as the Republic of Salò. He and his family were housed at the Villa Feltrinelli in Gargnano under the strict supervision of the SS., until the RSI came to an end in April 1945.

In Salò today, there is hardly anything to remind you that the Nazis staged their Italian shadow regime from here. This is mainly because they built very few new structures for their facilities, but rather repurposed the existing buildings.

To help people understand the events of the period, interpretive signage has been installed at those locations where the political events of the time unfolded. A map points out seventeen principal buildings and explains in detail what function they originally served and how they were used in the time of the RSI. Only from this perspective does the complex organizational structure of the puppet state become clear.

Along the waterfront, it is difficult to miss the imposing Palazzo della Magnifica Patria with its open portico on the ground floor. It served as the seat of the *Comunità di Riviera*, an administrative unit for 34 municipalities along the western and southern shores of Lake Garda founded in 1334, and was redesigned in 1560 under Venetian rule.

On the building's rear facade there is a placard explaining that from 1943 to 1945 it was used as an office for state interpreters. Today it is again reborn as Salò's city hall.

Address Municipio (Palazzo della Magnifica Patria), Lungolago Zanardelli 52, 25087 Salò (BS) | Getting there From the SS 45, drive in the direction of Salò Centro. Parking is available in many places, including the city theater in Piazza San Bernardo. | Tip On the rear of the Municipio you will find a beautiful historic clock.

43__Isola del Garda
A dream in the middle of the lake

A trip to the Isola del Garda is positively enchanting. Even the crossing to the island, located off the headland of San Felice del Benaco, is a pleasure. From five departure points on the west side of the lake, including Gardone, Salò, and Manerba, the trip takes only 15 minutes; from Garda or Bardolino on the east shore, about a half hour. The Borghese-Cavazza family, which privately owns the island, has opened parts of the villa and the surrounding gardens to visitors since 2001.

The Isola del Garda, the largest of the five islands in Lake Garda, has a long history. It was populated during Roman times and served for more than 900 years as a Franciscan monastery before falling into private ownership in the 1800s.

The monastery's facade lit up the island at the end of the 19th century, thanks to the family of Duke Gaetano de Ferrari from Genoa, who commissioned the building of a magnificent villa in the neo-Gothic Venetian style, and landscaped the large gardens, extending the island, through landfill, on the western side. Through marriage, the island transferred to the Borghese family from Rome, and in 1927, it passed to Count Alessandro Cavazza from Bologna. Today, his daughter-in-law, Lady Chetwynd-Talbot, and her seven grown children manage the property. In addition to the villa and gardens, tourists can visit a campground with a boating center, vacation at an *agriturismo* (loosely translated as "farmhouse resort"), and see an olive plantation in San Felice del Benaco.

Alberta Borghese-Cavazza organizes tours of the site, which begin with the marvelously manicured gardens. Thanks to the particular microclimate of the island, a rich variety of Mediterranean vegetation, including palms, agave, and bougainvillea, thrives here. After a look in the rooms of the villa, tour goers take the opportunity to sip an aperitif on the terrace before continuing on through the island's romantic forest.

Address Azienda Agricola Borghese Cavazza Società Agricola, Via Mazzini 22, 25010 San Felice del Benaco (BS), Tel 0039/328/384/9226, info@isoladelgarda.com | **Getting there** Visit www.isoladelgarda.com for up-to-date information about departure points and times. | **Hours** Mar–Oct, visits and tours by appointment only | **Tip** From the small picturesque harbor at Portese you can take a stroll along the beautiful coast of the promontory and take in the 15th-century Chiesetta di San Fermo.

44__Fonte Boiola

Soaking your way to wellness

It's possible that the Romans knew about the Boiola thermal springs and used them to feed their baths with hot mineral-rich water. They are first mentioned in writing in the poem *Benacus*, published in 1546 by the monk Jodoco di Bergamo. It would have been hard not to notice the bubbles that rise from the lake some 1,000 feet eastward off the coast of Sirmione, leaving behind the powerful smell of sulfur. A Venetian diver first successfully tapped the Boiola springs in the year 1889.

Aboard a tour boat, you will usually see the small whirlpool where the Boiola springs emerge from the earth with their over-150-degree Fahrenheit water (about 70 degrees Celsius). That water today feeds several thermal spas in Sirmione: those at the treatment centers Terme Virgilio and Terme Catullo; at three hotels, Grand Hotel Terme, Hotel Sirmione, and Hotel Fonte Boiola; and the Centro Benessere Termale Aquaria, which opened in 2003. This new complex lies tucked away in a park at the northern end of the old city. An olive garden on its western edge by the lake is laid out as a large open-air swimming pool, so that while you practice your strokes in the pleasantly warm water you can enjoy an incredibly beautiful view over Lake Garda.

In front of the entrance to the Aquaria complex, a marble bust from 1914 commemorates one of the three men who made it all possible, namely Giuseppe Piana, who was successful in piping the thermal water into the first therapy facilities. Around the same time, Angelo Piatti worked on analyzing the sulfur, bromine, and iodine content in the water, and the hotelier Angelo Gennari began the first balneotherapy treatments in Sirmione.

The power of the soothing and healing thermal waters now attract up to 50,000 spa guests annually to the peninsula, and are primarily used therapeutically to treat respiratory diseases and rheumatism, though sometimes it's nice just to use them to enhance your *benessere*, or well-being.

AL COMM. G. PIANA
CARATTERE FIERO E TENACE
CHE CON DIFFICOLTÀ
E SACRIFICI
VOLLE E POTÉ CONDURRE
L'ACQUA TERMALE
DALLA SUA SORGENTE
NEL LAGO
ALLO STABILIMENTO DI CURA
DA LUI ERETTO
PROCURANDO SALUTE
A MOLTI AMMALATI
E PROSPERITÀ
A QUESTA PENISOLA
3 MAGGIO 1914

Address Centro Benessere Termale Aquaria, Piazza Don Piatti 1, 25019 Sirmione (BS), Tel 0039/030/916044, www.termedisirmione.com | **Getting there** From the SS 11, take the SP 13 toward Centro on the peninsula; you should park in the lot at the Scaligeri castle, as beyond lies a pedestrian zone. Hotel guests can drive to their lodging. | **Hours** Mar–Nov, Mon–Wed, Fri, and Sun 10am–11pm; Thurs and Sat 10am–midnight; because hours can change, we recommend calling for up-to-date information. | **Tip** On the way to the northern tip of the peninsula, a spur leads to the church of San Pietro in Mavino, founded in 765 by Lombard monks. There is a huge bell immediately adjacent, which is rung on specific dates to remember the fallen of the World Wars.

45___Gelateria Da Gino

Where the locals go for tradition and quality

Sirmione seems like it has the greatest number of ice-cream shops of any city around Lake Garda, and maybe even the world. They line the Via Vittorio Emanuele, one enticing *gelateria* after another, vying for customers with their colorful and delicious mountains of ice cream.

The residents of Sirmione don't have to think long when asked which *gelateria* they prefer: without question it's the one run by Gino Mancini, whose gelato parlor, with its neon-green lettering, lies between the two arches that span the main road. On three sides it opens out into a small outdoor seating area on the Piazza Flaminia. Here, the different flavors of gelato on offer are leveled evenly in their containers, and for good reason. Because they are made using only natural ingredients that would quickly melt, it isn't possible to have them protrude artfully from the tops of their containers.

The family knows its *mestiere* ("craft") very well. The tradition of this shop goes back further than any other in town. The uncle of the current owners, who had the common Sirmione surname of Catullo, started selling his homemade gelato in 1933. He did not have a storefront, only a small ice-cream cart. He had to give up his trade during the war, when ingredients were in short supply. His nephew Gino resumed the business in 1964, and still opens the shop early each morning in order to serve coffee to the people already going about their day.

Gino's sons maintain their father's tried-and-true methods for making the ice cream. Their raspberry sorbet gets its deep red color because it is made from 56 percent fruit pulp. For flavors such as *noce* (walnut) or *pistacchio*, only the best Piedmontese nuts and highest-quality pistachios are used.

The local favorite, *granita*, a treat that originated in Sicily and is similar to Italian ice, is made using only fresh fruits and is swirled constantly to maintain just the right consistency.

Address Piazza Flaminia 2, 25019 Sirmione (BS) | **Getting there** From the SS 11, take the SP 13 toward Centro on the peninsula; park in the lot at the Scaligeri Castle and walk through the pedestrianized city to Via Vittorio Emanuele. The *gelateria* will be on the left-hand side. | **Hours** Mid–Mar–Oct, Mon–Sun 6:30am until late; Nov–mid-March, Thurs–Tues 6:30am until late. Closed Wed. | **Tip** Most restaurants are concentrated on the two large squares that face west toward the lake, Piazza Castello and Piazza Carducci.

46___Grotte di Catullo

Ruins of an ancient Roman villa

It's easy to leave the hustle and bustle of the narrow streets of the old city behind as you walk from the Piazza Don Piatti through the olive groves out toward the waterfront. There, atop a hill at the northeastern tip of the peninsula, lie the Grotte di Catullo (Grottoes of Catullus), named by Marino Sanudo in his chronicles of 1483. The name is a bit misleading, however, because there are no caves to see here, but rather the ruins of a huge villa complex. And they have nothing at all to do with the famous Roman poet Gaius Valerius Catullus.

In any case, Gaius Valerius Catullus, who came from a wealthy Veronese family and lived in the first century B.C., must have been very comfortable in the Roman city of Sirmio, as Sirmione was then known. In his *Carmina 31* he writes: "Sirmio, jewel of islands and of peninsulas, Whatever each Neptune carries, In the calm clear waters and in the vast sea, How gladly and how happy I see you!" He follows that passage with the oft quoted *Salve, o venusta Sirmio* ("Hail, beautiful Sirmio"). It is believed that his family did own a summer villa here, though not in this location.

Sanudo originally referred to the site as a grotto because of its collapsing walls, which gave it the feel of an overgrown cave. What presents itself here, however, is actually the relic of a first-century building. The former three-story complex probably served as a *mansio*, or state guesthouse, and extends on a site more than 550 feet long by 340 feet wide.

Passing through the museum, which provides a historical reconstruction of the site and parts of its magnificent facilities, you enter into the excavation area surrounded by groves of ancient olive trees. On the long sides ran covered porches, joined in the north by a terrace built on massive substructures. Through each of the terrace's archways, you can enjoy a new panoramic view out over turquoise-blue waters of the lake.

Address Piazzale Orti Manara 4, 25019 Sirmione (BS), Tel 0039/030/916157 | **Getting there** Take the SP13 toward Centro on the peninsula; park at the Scaligeri castle and walk through the pedestrianized city, following signs to the Piazza Don Piatti. | **Hours** Apr–Oct, Tues–Sat 8:30am–7:30pm, Sun 8:30am–6:30pm; Nov–Mar, Tues–Sat 8:30am–5pm, Sun 8:30am–2pm (Ticket office closes 30 minutes prior) | **Tip** If you want to save your strength for the tour, you should take the original electric train from the 1960s, which runs regularly between the Piazza Don Piatti and the Grottoes of Catullus.

47 _ Rocca Scaligera
A bird's-eye view from the battlements

If you were to ask a child to draw a castle, you would probably get something that looks a lot like the Scaligeri castle in Sirmione: a wall with three towers, two at the corners and a taller one in the center, everything crowned with battlements. Yet despite its archetypal shape, this is quite possibly the most unique of all the Scaligeri castles in the region. First, it is built directly over the water, and second, it is the entryway to the historic city of Sirmione.

After driving about a mile and a half down the narrow peninsula's coastal road, you'll see the castle standing ceremoniously before you. Cars are not allowed beyond this point, and the only way into town is over a channel. The castle stands guard over the waterway with a drawbridge, and so the arch through the bulwark becomes the proverbial eye of the needle through which everyone coming into Sirmione must pass.

For those not interested in museums or art exhibitions, the castle is a must-see; for here, the architecture and the sweeping views are the biggest draws. From the main courtyard visitors can ascend a steel staircase in the corner tower to explore the walls of the 13th-century castle. If you can, it's well worth your while to continue climbing to the top of the 155-foot-tall central tower, or *mastio*, where a panoramic view of the site and the town of Sirmione beyond unfolds before you.

Mastino I della Scala commissioned the building of the castle in 1277, and the southern courtyard and outer walls were added in the 14th century.

The castle's protected harbor, larger in area itself than the entire building complex, took shape in 1405 under the Venetians, who used it to control commerce on the lake. Seagulls have now taken up positions on the battlements, and from the same bird's-eye perspective you can gaze with them out over the turquoise-blue waters of Lake Garda.

Address Piazza Castello 4, 25019 Sirmione (BS) | **Getting there** From the SS 11, take the SP 13 toward Centro on the peninsula; it's best to park in the lot at the Scaligeri castle, as beyond is a pedestrian zone. | **Hours** Apr–Sep, Mon–Sun 9am–7pm; Oct–Mar, Tues–Sun 9am–4pm | **Tip** Stop in to see the frescoes in the small church of Sant'Anna, directly across from the entrance to the Scaligeri castle.

48_ Shaka Surf Center
Putting the wind in your sails

A strong wind blows down from Malcesine, and you can see it shooting windsurfers and paragliders at high speeds over the lake and filling the sails of the innumerable boats on the water. Even when docked in the harbours, their tall masts pitch furiously back and forth.

Boats have always been important here. It was not always feasible to build a road between Malcesine and Torbole, as evidenced by the many tunnels and the piles of fallen rocks along the Gardesana Orientale. Its construction was only made possible in 1929 by extensive blasting and modern technology. Prior to this, visitors to Lake Garda would have had to board a boat in Torbole to continue traveling south.

The borders of the provinces of Verona, Brescia, and Trento all converge here at the northern tip of the lake, and there is a roughly seven-square-mile area of water within the borders of Trento, extending from just south of Torbole across to just north of Limone, that is closed to motor boats, making it an ideal spot for windsurfing. The best conditions on the lake are found here, especially when the *ora* wind begins to blow in the early afternoon.

Recently the Shaka Surf Center, at the southern end of Torbole, has become the bustling epicenter of the surfing community. People pull their boards from the roofs of their cars or are fitted out with rentals. Windsurfers enter the water from a large lakeside terrace covered in artificial turf, and very quickly they are only visible by their large, colorful sails. If you're not feeling up to it, you can just chill out on the large cushions listening to music.

Those who are a little less adventurous or athletically inclined can also consider taking out a stand-up paddleboard in the morning hours when the water is still and calm. Though it's a much slower ride, you can still get a feel for what it's like to skim along the surface of the lake.

Address Via Lungolago Conca d'Oro 12, 38069 Torbole (TN), Tel 0039/0464/506347, www.shakasurfcenter.com | **Getting there** Follow the signs to the parking lot of the Surf Center from the SR 249. | **Hours** Mar–Nov, from mornings to late afternoons | **Tip** There are various hiking trails that radiate out from Torbole, including the *Marmitte dei Giganti* ("giants' potholes"), created by glacial deposits.

49__ Calderini Memorial

Homage to a son of the city

There are many facets to Torri del Benaco. The picturesque scenery of the town includes buildings with pastel-colored facades and arch-spanned alleyways, as well as the stately palaces that are testament to the town's immense wealth and to the significant role it played in the history of the region.

A fine example of these important structures is the Palazzo della Gardesana, along the harbor.

Under the Venetian Republic from 1405 to 1797, this grand building was the seat of the Consiglio della Gardesana dell'Acqua, a union of cities from around Lake Garda that established water laws, stringent taxes, and controlled commerce on the water. At the beginning of their meetings, the council members attended mass in the small church of the Santissima Trinità, and afterward held their discussions in the palace, located directly next door. These days, it has been repurposed as a hotel and full-service restaurant.

Before the first archway of the loggia stands a tall rectangular marble slab. A long paragraph is chiseled into its front, and it is crowned with a coat of arms encircled by a half shell. It remembers Domizio Calderini, who was born here in 1444 and succumbed to the plague in Rome at the age of 34. His father, Antonio, had the memorial erected with an inscription that traces the life of his son: after studying liberal arts in Verona, he went to Rome and distinguished himself serving as a translator of the languages of classical antiquity to Pope Sixtus IV, revealing to all the secrets of the poets and philosophers.

Domizio Calderini was indeed revered in Italy as one of the most admired scholars of his time. It was the influence of his father, who served as notary for the Gardesana dell'Acqua and therefore also lived in this palazzo, that provided him with this memorial stone, so that every visitor to Torri del Benaco today pays his respects to the noted humanist.

Address Albergo Ristorante Gardesana, Piazza Domizio Calderini 5, 37010 Torri del Benaco (VR), Tel 0039/045/7225411 | **Getting there** From the SR 249, a large parking lot is located immediately south of the Scaligeri Castle. | **Tip** There are many restaurants and bars around the harbor that invite you to linger and take in the tranquil setting.

50__ The Scaligeri Castle
Picturesque scenery with a limonaia

The dynasty of the Scaliger family could easily be described as construction-happy. During their 110-year rule between 1277 and 1387, they built up Verona as the capital of their empire with several palaces and the Castelvecchio. Additionally, they erected several enormous residences throughout their territory along Lake Garda to demonstrate their power and military might. These indomitable fortresses can be seen from Riva in the north through Malcesine, Torri del Benaco, Lazise, and Sirmione in the south.

Visiting each of these castles is a unique experience, due to the special way their design was influenced by their particular location and context.

In Torri del Benaco, for example, the fortress was conceived with the security of the adjacent harbor and lakeshore in mind, and is therefore oriented at right angles to the water.

The ruins of the citadel of Berengar I stood on this spot when Antonio della Scala commissioned the castle's construction in 1383. Today the building operates as an ethnographic museum with nine rooms dedicated to life in the Lake Garda region. The olive-oil manufacturing industry is represented by such traditional equipment as a transport carriage for the harvested fruit and a small press used in the home. The work of the fishermen and boatbuilders is represented by a Lake Garda gondola and various kinds of nets.

While most of the objects belong firmly rooted in the past, the traditional *limonaia*, or lemon greenhouse, situated along the castle's southern wall and originally constructed in 1760, is still functioning today.

Handsome lemon trees thrive behind its sun-warmed walls. Slightly inclined irrigation channels bring the water collected behind small dams to the rows of trees. Even the goldfish and turtles swimming contently in these pools of water seem to appreciate their idyllic surroundings.

Address Viale Fratelli Lavanda 2, 37010 Torri del Benaco (VR), Tel 0039 / 045 / 6296111,
www.museodelcastelloditorridelbenaco.it | **Getting there** From the SR 249, a large
parking lot is located immediately south of the Scaligeri castle. | **Hours** Apr 1–June 15,
9:30am–12:30pm and 2:30–6pm; June 16–Sep 15, 9:30am–1pm and 4:30–7:30pm;
Sep 16–Oct 31, 9:30am–12:30pm and 2:30–6pm; Nov–Mar, closed. | **Tip** A serpentine
road leads from here to Dorf Albisano, which Gabriele d'Annunzio referred to as
"Lake Garda's Balcony" thanks to its breathtaking view.

51 — The Tower of Berengar I
Sanctuary of the first king of Italy

Just the translation of Torri del Benaco's name – "towers of Lake Garda" – conjures up images of the many fortified buildings dotting the landscape. What time period this name recalls, however, can only be found after exploring the area.

The immense crenellated towers of the imposing Scaligeri castle are prominently visible throughout the town. In the middle of the old city lies the powerful Torre dell'Orologio, with a clock on its facade and a small belfry. During the Middle Ages, this tower housed the *Vicinia*, an assembly of the town's leading families who dealt with the affairs of the community, and was also used as a storehouse for the taxes paid in goods rather than money.

In the Piazza della Chiesa, you'll finally come upon the tower that gave the town its Latin moniker, *Castrum Turrium*, as late as the 10th century. This defiant structure is the Tower of Berengar. Constructed of rough limestone blocks on a square base, it is the only one remaining of the four original defensive towers of the old citadel, called the Trincerò.

With the fall of the Kingdom of the Franks, the Huns began to invade northern Italy, and the Lombards reacted by building defensive towers with the aim of banding together and creating a united Italian kingdom.

In the year 888, Berengar I was crowned the first king of Italy. He had the citadel built at Torri, and portions of its wall are still visible today. His rule was broken several times, however, and after being crowned king for the third time in the year 905, he once again set his sights on Torri.

A marble tablet, affixed to the tower on the 1,000th anniversary of his death on November 4, 1924, remembers the occasion when Berengar, after defeating Ludovico III of Bourgogne and recovering his kingdom, wrote out six certificates rewarding those who helped lead him to victory.

Address Vicolo Chiesa 7, 37010 Torri del Benaco (VR) | **Getting there** From the SR 249, a large parking lot is located immediately south of the Scaligeri Castle. | **Hours** Not open to the public | **Tip** The Baroque church of Saints Peter and Paul stands next to the tower along the Piazza della Chiesa, which opens out to the lake.

52 __ Car Ferries
A crossing from Torri del Benaco

A boat trip on Lake Garda is a must for any visitor to the region. The only vessel operating all year round is currently the car ferry between Toscolano-Maderno and Torri del Benaco. Every day from around 8am until 8pm, the *traghetto* shuttles vehicles and passengers in 35-minute trips back and forth between the western and eastern shores of the lake. Depending on traffic, there are sometimes two ferries in operation. The regular rhythm of the boats is interrupted only by the midday break, still obligatory in Italy.

It's worthwhile crossing by ferry, as otherwise driving would re-quire a rather lengthy circumnavigation of the lake to reach Torri del Benaco. From here up to Riva del Garda and on to the other side of the lake is about 56 miles, and it is almost 50 heading in a southerly direction toward Sirmione.

In addition, the ferry crosses the lake at a topographically inter-esting spot. At this point, the lake is still quite narrow, and directly to the south it begins expanding into a wide basin. The landscape changes correspondingly, and you can see the mountains taper out into the broad plains.

It's a win-win situation: while the refreshing breeze ripples through your hair as you stand on the boat's deck, you can get a true feel for the full expanse of the beautiful lake. There are sights to see at both ends of the ride, so it doesn't matter which direction you travel in – either towards the Scaligeri castle in Torri del Benaco, or the stately parish church of San Ercolano, close to the ferry dock in Maderno.

Between June and October, a second car ferry operates between Limone and Malcesine. If you would rather cover the entire expanse of Lake Garda, there is a fast hydrofoil that runs between Peschiera, Desenzano, and Riva del Garda. Better still is a leisurely circuit aboard one of the small passenger ships that call at all major towns around the lake.

Address Via Lungolago Zanardelli (above Hotel Milano, Via Lungolago Zanardelli 12), 25088 Toscolano-Maderno (BS) | **Getting there** Follow signs to the ferry dock from the SS 45 in Maderno. | **Hours** Current departure times can be found at www.navigazionelaghi.it; schedules can also be obtained at jetties all around the lake. | **Tip** Among the row of buildings facing the lake in Maderno, the beautiful church of San Andrea stands out, a masterpiece of First Romanesque architecture.

53_Museo della Carta

A walk through the history of paper-making

Toscolano-Maderno combines two historic villages into one municipal authority. The historic dividing line between the two towns was the swift-moving river called the Toscolano. In the 14th century, along its banks grew the paper manufacturing industry, which became the economic lifeblood of the city over the next several centuries. Even major printers moved from Venice to be closer to their suppliers. The trade gradually fell victim to industrialization in the 19th century, and the last mill finally closed its doors in the 1960s.

The few remaining craftsmen did not want to let the meaningful history of the industry get lost to the ages. They set into action establishing a special project for the redevelopment of the mills into an *ecomuseo*, a special eco-friendly museum, showcasing the importance of the *Valle delle Cartiere*, or valley of the paper mills.

A bridge over the wild stream leads to the mountain slope where the Museo della Carta ("paper museum") is located. Those who expect to find a run-of-the-mill exhibition explaining the logging industry will soon realize how mistaken they are. Even the entry path itself, which runs along the stream and offers views of the ruins of the mills, is part of the museum concept. Interpretive signage illustrates the history of the industry, and points out the special flora found in the scenic valley – such as ferns or the carnivorous butterwort – that covers the humid rock face.

The factory buildings of the former Maina Inferiore paper mill, with its tall smokestack, are surrounded by the old living quarters of the factory managers and millworkers. An exhibit showcasing the historical tools of the trade has been curated to explain the paper-manufacturing process in great detail, including the indispensable role played by the water. There are also printing presses on display that were used in the 15th and 16th centuries, when this area was the center of paper manufacturing in the Venetian Republic.

Address Museo della Carta di Toscolano-Maderno, Via Valle delle Cartiere, 25088 Toscolano-Maderno (BS), Tel 0039/0365/546023, www.valledellecartiere.it | **Getting there** Park on the bridge (on the SS45) and go by foot, or drive a bit farther to the parking lot at the old *Quattroruote* paper mill. | **Hours** Varies somewhat each year; Apr–mid-May, Sat–Sun 10am–6pm; mid-May–late Sep, Mon–Sun 10am–6pm; Oct, 10am to 6pm | **Tip** There is a bar in the old Maina Inferiore mill where you can build up your strength for the waterside walk.

54__Nodi d'Amore

A pasta specialty that celebrates a legend

Pasta has simply been an indispensible – and beloved – part of the Italian diet for centuries. The creativity of Italian cooks is shown through the enormous variety of different types of pasta and regional pasta specialties found throughout the country. In addition to the more than 350 kinds of dried pastas, there is *pasta all'uovo*, fresh pasta made with eggs, and also filled pastas, like agnolotti, ravioli, tortellini, and the thicker tortelloni. Pasta makers in Valeggio sul Mincio pride themselves on a unique local signature dish, the *nodi d'amore*, or love knots: tortellini filled with various kinds of meat, vegetables, and seasonings.

The nodi d'amore recall a local legend: at the end of the 1300s, the Milanese ruler Gian Galeazzo Visconti camped with his troops along the banks of the river Mincio. In the camp, a jester shared a story about how the river was populated by lovely nymphs who emerged at night to dance, but that a curse made them appear as horrible ugly witches.

That night the witches emerged and began to dance among the sleeping soldiers. The captain of the guard, Malco, stayed awake to see, and grabbed hold of one of them. While wriggling to free herself, the witch lost her cloak, revealing the beautiful nymph, Silvia. The two fell head-over-heels in love, and the nymph gave Malco a golden handkerchief before returning to the water.

The next night during a celebration, Malco recognized Silvia disguised among the dancers. The glances that the two exchanged ignited jealousy in Isabella, a noblewoman in love with Malco, who denounced Silva. The guards went to arrest her, but Malco allowed her to escape.

As Malco sat imprisoned that night, the captain was visited by Silvia, who proposed escaping into the river together. They made their way to the Mincio, leaving behind only a gold silk handkerchief knotted by the two lovers to signify their love.

Address *Nodi d'amore* is available at many restaurants and markets, including the Pastificio Remelli in the city center, Via Alessandro Sala 30, 37067 Valeggio sul Mincio (VR), Tel 0039/045/7951630 | **Hours** Mon 2:30–7:30pm, Tues–Fri 8:30am–12:30pm and 2:30–7:30pm, Sat 8:30am–12:30pm | **Tip** Every year in mid-June, the *Festa del nodo d'amore* takes place in Valeggio sul Mincio, when the 2,000-foot-long Visconti bridge over the river turns into an open air restaurant.

55__Parco Giardino Sigurtà

Exploring the park and gardens by golf cart

The 150-acre Parco Giardino Sigurtà rightly advertises with the slogan: *una meraviglia unica al mondo*, "a unique marvel of the world." In 2013, it was named the most beautiful park in Italy for the second time. The park has also had many illustrious visitors, including Prince Charles and Margaret Thatcher.

The gardens sprawl with an enormous assortment of rambling lawns interspersed with flowerbeds blooming with tulips, irises, roses, and asters (depending on the season), a walled area with a game enclosure, and 17 ornamental ponds and lakes surrounded by romantic and poetic squares.

The idea for the park goes back to Doctor Carlo Sigurtà, who purchased the property while on a chance visit to Valeggio in 1941. Ownership of the land included rights to draw water from the Mincio River, which enabled him to breathe life into the grounds, combining the historic 17th-century *parco*, with its mature trees, and the new *giardino*, with its flowers and other decorative flora. Carlo Sigurtà opened the park to visitors in March 1978, and today his descendants, Conti Giuseppe and Magda Inga Sigurtà manage the property. It is still privately owned, and its upkeep and maintenance are financed through entry fees and private events.

In order to explore the park in its entirety (without endurance training, that is), you can sign up for a guided tour aboard a small train or bus, ride a bike, or wind about yourself on a GPS-enabled golf cart, a special treat that can't be recommended too highly. You can zip along the charming Viale delle Rose, the park's main attraction. The small roadway is lined with colorful blooming rosebushes and is in constant view of the Scaligeri castle in Valeggio sul Mincio, which seems so within reach that you'd almost think it was within the park itself.

From the forested areas, there is another special vista down into the village in the valley of the Mincio River.

Address Via Cavour 1, 37067 Valeggio sul Mincio (VR), Tel 0039/045/6371033, www.sigurta.it | **Getting there** The SR 249 leads from Peschiera to Valeggio sul Mincio; there is a large parking lot close by on Via Baden Powell. | **Hours** Varies somewhat each year; Mar and Oct, Mon–Sun 9am–6pm; Apr–Sept, Mon–Sun 9am–7pm (Ticket office closes one hour prior) | **Tip** Nearby in the idyllic little town of Dorf Borghetto, with its narrow alleys and water mills on the Mincio, you'll think you've been transported back to the Middle Ages.

56__Antica Bottega del Vino

A wine selection that's tough to beat

Almost hidden in a small alley just a few steps off of the Via Mazzini lies the Antica Bottega del Vino, which advertises itself as the *tempio del vino,* or temple of wine. An old sign and burning lanterns lit during business hours draw your attention to the old *vinoteca* hidden behind the large, dark leaded door. As you enter, you'll be surprised by the enormous height and spaciousness of its rooms. The loud clamor of voices at the bar and the wine bottles lining the yellow plastered walls make a lively first impression.

This watering hole has been around since 1890, and in 2010 it passed into the ownership of the twelve "Amarone Families," all wine producers from around the region.

The front area retains the rustic charm of the old *vinoteca*. Chalkboards by the bar display the nearly 40 wines available by the glass, which visitors can enjoy while seated at the dark black wooden tables. Locals frequently meet here to catch up over a glass of wine, giving tourists the feeling that they've been allowed into the homes of the Veronese.

A full-service restaurant occupies the rooms at the back of the building. The menu offers local specialties such as *risotto all'Amarone, gnocchi al pomodoro, pasta e fagioli, risi e bisi,* and a hearty horsemeat goulash reminiscent of the traditional dishes of the surrounding countryside. The award-winning wine list offers around 3,000 options from around the world to choose from, all stored in the building's impressive cellars.

The logo of the *bottega* ("shop") depicts a half man, half two-tailed fish from the ancient world. This *gobbo*, or hunchback, hangs in the middle of bar and serves as a type of *portafortuna*, or good-luck charm, together with an image of the Madonna. After the Second World War, the *bottega* remained standing among many destroyed buildings in the neighborhood. To keep their luck alive, the owners still keep two small flames burning around the clock.

Address Via Scudo di Francia 3, 37121 Verona, Tel 0039 / 045 / 8004535, info@anticabottegadelvino.net | **Public Transit** Bus 70 to the Piazza Erbe stop; Bus 96, 97 to the Lungadige Rubele stop | **Hours** Mon – Sun 12–11pm | **Tip** The nearby Via Mazzini, lined with clothing stores, is a good spot for a shopping spree.

57__Arche Scaligere

A tomb under the watchful eye of a dog

The coat of arms of the della Scala family, also known as the Scaligeri, depicts a ladder (*scala* is the Italian word for "ladder"). Cangrande I della Scala's first name translates as "big dog," and this is illustrated on his canopy gravestone. Two crowned four-legged friends sit to the right and left of his sarcophagus and proudly hold a shield that bears the ladder of the family coat of arms in their paws.

The memorial monument was built in 1329 in a courtyard of the small church of Santa Maria Antica.

On a raised platform and built in the shape of a Gothic tabernacle, there are two more impressive marble tombs known as the Arche Scaligere, namely that of Mastino II and Cansignorio della Scala. Small Gothic enclosures protecting the tombs depict the merits and virtues of the rulers through decorative figures and ornaments. As with the tomb of Cangrande, the departed are portrayed as lying in repose atop the sarcophagi. They appear one further time in the prime of life and full of activity in an equestrian statue on the top of the pyramidal roof.

You can barely recognize Cangrande on his horse, he rises so high into the air. Since 1909, a copy has stood in place of the original statue, which was moved to the Museo del Castelvecchio in order to protect it from the elements. Cangrande was apparently so enamored of his namesake that he wore a helmet in the shape of a winged dog. Here the smiling rider has removed the helmet from his head. His sword is also stuck safely in its sheath, symbolizing times of peace, which were heralded by his victorious battles. He was able to expand his kingdom from Verona far to the east, including Belluno and Treviso all the way to Padua. The horse indeed also wears its original headdress – with a little winged dog.

For an up-close view of the statue, consider a visit to the museum on Corso Castelvecchio.

Address Via Arche Scaligere 3, 37121 Verona | **Public Transit** Bus 70 to the Piazza
Viviani stop; Bus 96, 97 to the Lungadige Rubele stop | **Hours** June–Oct, Tues–Sun
10am–1pm and 2–6pm; the rest of the year only by appointment | **Tip** A spectacular
walk by way of the Via Arche Scaligere leads to the Casa di Romeo and across the
Piazzetta Pescheria, ending on the bank of the Adige River.

58__Arco dei Gavi
The fate of the ancient triumphal arch

The triumphal arch of the Gavi family was erected at the beginning of the 1st century A.D. just outside the Roman city walls, on the Via Postumia. It was one of many memorial monuments that once lined the large overland roads leading to Cremona and Genoa. The footprint of Verona grew toward the south over the following centuries, and between 1194 and 1224, a new protective wall was built from one riverbank to the other, thereby securing the city lying in the bend of the Adige River. This new fortification incorporated the Arco dei Gavi as a city gate, standing near the clock tower of the Castelvecchio.

During the Renaissance, the triumphal arch received a new and special appreciation because a certain Lucius Vitruvius Cerdo was named as the architect in its inscription (which is no longer legible). People believed that this could identify him as the ancient architectural theorist and master builder Vitruvius, to whom the only surviving ancient treatise on building construction is attributed. Doubts were first raised by the Renaissance architect Serlio, however, who, in 1540, pictured the arch in his third book, where he points out that the great builder was named Vitruvius Pollio, and that design details of the Gavi arch were not in keeping with those laid out in Pollio's treatise.

The arch is made of white marble and follows the classical triaxial construction. It is divided by four fluted Corinthian half columns, with the two middle columns supporting a triangular pediment above the arch.

The Arco dei Gavi had already been damaged in the 16th century, was then further hit during the French occupation, and was dismantled in 1805. In 1932, the arch was reconstructed using the surviving pieces based on the drawings of Andrea Palladio. Since then, the Arco dei Gavi has stood intact, occupying its own little "parklet."

Address Corso Cavour (adjacent to the Castelvecchio), 37121 Verona | **Public Transit**
Bus 21, 22, 23, 24, 31, 32, 33, 41, 42, 61, 62, 91, 94, 95 to the Corso Castelvecchio
stop | **Tip** Be sure to check out the beautiful inner courtyard of the Palazzo Canossa,
located just four doors away to the right of the arch.

59__Arco della Costa
The weather forecast, according to a whalebone

A curious object, vaguely reminiscent of a cane, can be seen hanging from the first archway over the Via della Costa, the main road running from the Piazza delle Erbe to the Piazza dei Signori. The name of the arch, Arco della Costa, provides a bit of hint, as *costa* means "rib" in Italian. In fact, this is a rib bone from a large whale. But how did it get here, and why would it be suspended from this very conspicuous location?

In a detailed depiction of the city from the eighteenth century, the whalebone is already visible at this very spot. It may even have been there long before then, as the Arco della Costa, which also served as a pedestrian bridge connecting the two adjacent buildings, was built in the early 15th century. Judicial officers of the Venetian government could cross directly from their residence in the Domus Nova over the elevated pathway to the courthouse in the Palazzo della Ragione, thereby avoiding malice and bribery attempts in the streets below.

The whalebone dates from the end of the last ice age and was probably found in Verona. The huge fossil, which at one time people thought must have belonged to a mysterious monster, was put on display. Some looked at it as merely a curiosity, while others believed it could protect the center of Verona from disaster. Similar bones hang in the cathedral and in the northern side chapel of the church of Sant'Anastasia for the same reason. There is even a legend that the bone will fall on the head of the first person to pass beneath it who has never told a lie.

Today, many people of Verona still consider the enigmatic *costa* to be a great omen. They believe that the fossil can predict the weather: If the bone hangs parallel to the arch, good weather is in store for the city; if it turns, then the opposite is true, and *tempo brutto*, or ugly weather, lies ahead. You can therefore forgo the local weather report and instead just take heed of the Arco della Costa.

Address Piazza delle Erbe / Via della Costa, 37121 Verona | Public Transit Bus 70 to the Piazza Erbe stop; Bus 96, 97 to the Lungadige Rubele stop | Tip The remarkable courtyard of the Palazzo della Ragione is still called the Mercato Vecchio, because small shops once stood here in the buttresses.

60_ The Arena

Opera beneath the moonlight

Verona's amphitheater is called the Arena, and is the third largest in Italy after those in Rome and Capua. It is the only one, however, that continues to regularly stage performances, honoring its original purpose. Opera season runs from June to September, and showcases mainly classics by Giuseppe Verdi such as *Aida*, *Nabucco*, and *La Traviata*. In addition, visitors can tour this magnificent structure throughout the year.

The amphitheater was built out of white and pink limestone from Valpolicella in 30 A.D., outside the walls of the Roman city, and was incorporated into its expansion in 265 A.D. In 1117, an earthquake destroyed most of the outer ring of the Arena, and only four buttresses on three floors remain; citizens of Verona refer to this area as *l'ala* ("the wing"). In the Middle Ages, the building was basically used as a marble quarry, and many of its large blocks of stone can be seen repurposed in buildings such as the Castelvecchio.

Reconstruction of the Arena began during the Renaissance. The structure could originally accommodate 28,000 people for games and competitions, far more than the approximately 10,000 city residents of the time, and is now considered the largest open-air opera house in the world, attracting nearly 20,000 spectators to each performance.

Outside of the Arena on the spacious Piazza Bra, people begin to gather before the start of every show around nine o'clock. When it's time to be seated, the ingenuity of the Romans proves to have withstood the test of time, as visitors reach their seats easily over various vaulted walkways and gates, from the expensive inner ring up to the *gradinate*, the seating on the sloped stone steps. Regardless of where you're sitting, the acoustics are extraordinary. The audiences' enthusiasm grows as the elaborately costumed opera singers, the choir, masses of extras, and the occasional live animal take to the gigantic stage under the moonlit skies of Verona.

Address Piazza Bra, 37121 Verona, Tel 0039/045/8003204, www.arena.it | **Public Transit** Bus 11, 12, 13, 72, 90, 92, 93, 96, 97, 98, 510 to the Piazza Bra stop | **Hours** Tours are available Mon 1:45–7:30pm and Tues–Sun 8:30am–7:30pm (ticket office closes at 6:45pm); during the summer opera season times may change. | **Tip** At the Piazza Mura Gallieno, you can see more of the remains of the city walls – built in the year 265 by Gallienus – into which the Arena was incorporated.

61_ The Baptistery
San Giovanni in Fonte and its artistic treasure

The church of San Giovanni in Fonte is only accessible through the interior of the Cattedrale di Santa Maria Assunta, Verona's cathedral. Beneath the huge organ, a door opens out to the atrium, and from there you will be guided to the adjoining baptistery.

In the church dedicated to John the Baptist, visitors are in for a real treat: An enormous octagonal baptismal font with a diameter of nearly ten feet stands at the center of the nave. The font, which was carved at the end of the 13th century from a single block of Veronese marble, is considered a masterpiece of Romanesque sculpture.

Scenes with expressive high-relief figures adorn its eight outer sides, framed by pillars and arched friezes. The realistic scenes seem to practically burst with life, telling the story of Jesus, beginning with the Annunciation, which visitors will see directly in front of them as they enter. Mary leans frightened against a throne while the angel in a flowing robe hangs suspended above her with his wings spread wide. The biblical story unfolds further around the font with the Visitation and the Birth, the Annunciation to the Shepherds, and the Adoration of the Magi. Next comes the depiction of King Herod's command for the Massacre of the Innocents, and then the Flight into Egypt, with the Baptism of Christ rounding out the sequence.

The last scene with John the Baptist points to the original function of the building as the baptistery of the cathedral. It was built in 1123 after a previous iteration was destroyed by an earthquake in 1117.

During the recent restoration in 2005 it was revealed that in the past, the water was cleared in an underground basin before it flowed into the baptismal font. Presumably there was a direct connection to a water line, which dates back even further, to the time of the Romans, whose thermal baths once occupied this site.

Address Piazza Duomo, 37121 Verona | **Public Transit** Bus 70 to the Piazza Duomo stop; Bus 96, 97 to the Lungadige San Giorgio stop | **Hours** Mar–Oct, Mon–Sat 9am–5:30pm, Sun 1:30–5:30pm; Nov–Feb, Mon–Sat 10am–5pm, Sun 10am–4pm | **Tip** In the Caffè Duomo, Piazza Duomo 4, you can sit splendidly in a small garden.

62 Casa di Romeo

The fabled residence of the Montague Family

Verona is known the world over as the setting of William Shakespeare's most famous tragedy, *Romeo and Juliet*. Everyone can identify with the romantic but ill-fated love story, it seems. The only people who have difficulty doing so are the Veronese themselves, because they know that Shakespeare never visited Verona, and that his 1597 play is purely a work of fiction.

A kernel of truth does lie in the details of the story, however. In the first half of the 14th century, the Guelphs and Ghibellines, respectively supporters of the Pope and the emperor, were engaged in a long-standing feud here in the city. The existence of the Montecchi and Capuleti families, upon which it is speculated the Montagues and Capulets were based, can also be confirmed, though there is no proof that they were rivals. The house of the Capuleti was easily identifiable by the coat of arms bearing a hat, or *cappello* in Italian, from which their name is derived.

A nearby house was simply designated as the home of the Montecchi merchant family. Casa di Romeo is one of the few remaining typical residences in Verona dating from the Middle Ages with a crenellated wall along the street enclosing a courtyard, behind which lies the house itself.

Next to the arched entry, two quotes have been inscribed from Act I, Scene I of Shakespeare's famous text. Lady Montague asks, "Oh, where is Romeo?" before falling silent after hearing that her son hasn't (yet) been caught up in a violent fight with the Capulets. And Romeo, already desperately in love with Juliet, laments, "Tut, I have lost myself. I am not here. This is not Romeo. He's some other where."

Unlike the house of Juliet (see page 162), the alleged home of the Bard's young hero is not open to the public and can only be viewed from the street, leaving what lies beyond its imposing doorway up to the imagination of the beholder.

Address Via Arche Scaligere 4, 37121 Verona | **Public Transit** Bus 70 to the Piazza Viviani stop; Bus 96, 97 to the Lungadige Rubele stop | **Hours** Not open to the public | **Tip** In the house next door you'll find the Osteria al Duca, where affordable and delicious Veronese home cooking is offered in a rustic atmosphere.

63__Case Mazzanti

Self-promoting frescoes with a moral

The Case Mazzanti on the northern side of the Piazza delle Erbe was named for its 16th-century residents, and is one of the city's finest examples of a decoratively painted building. When the sun shines on its broad facade, the luminosity and colors of its faded frescoes begin to unfold.

You have to strain your eyes somewhat to read the inscriptions. One names the artist, Alberto Cavalli from Mantua, who completed the paintings in 1530. The others name the patron and detail his intentions: *matthevs mazzantvs patriae ornamento svi et svuorum ac bene gvberna(n)tivm comodo f(ieri) i(ussit).* The inscriptions explain that Matteo Mazzanti – who constructed the house at the beginning of the 16th century – commissioned these paintings as a decoration for his hometown and for his family, but also to inspire good government.

However, the very prominent public location of these frescoes on the main square of Verona suggests that self-promotion was more likely the decisive motive.

In reality, these are a group of separate houses that were unified through the facade paintings. On the ground floor, bars and restaurants have moved into the old storefronts under the loggia. On the third floor you can see the painted stone walls in the narrow intervals and the figurative representations in the larger areas between the windows. The fluid and radiating painted figures are all connected as moral allegories.

The image at the center of the low houses prominently stands out as you gaze upon the frescoes. The nude female figure sitting blindfolded among open books and lively cupids can probably be better understood as a symbol of ignorance, of someone who does not perceive, or perhaps does not try to perceive, her great fortune. She seems to still speak to today's viewers, encouraging us to always keep our eyes open to the world around us.

Address Piazza delle Erbe 1, 37121 Verona | **Public Transit** Bus 70 to the Piazza Erbe stop; Bus 96, 97 to the Lungadige Rubele stop | **Tip** The Caffè Filippini, a traditional meeting place for locals, is in the basement of the Case Mazzanti and contains both a bar and a full-service restaurant.

64__ Castel San Pietro

A breathtaking view over Verona

The Veronese love taking day trips on the weekend. When you are pressed for time, the Castel San Pietro offers a great destination right within the city limits, perched high atop the ring of hills along the Adige River. While you can certainly get there by car, mountaineering skills are by no means necessary to make the trip on foot. The former military building, located here for its strategically opportune position, offers today's visitors a breathtaking sight from a special perspective.

Starting at the Ponte Pietra, the Vicolo Botte and the Scalone Castel San Pietro lead directly up to the castle. Shaded by the greenery of small private gardens, the pathway takes you high up over winding stone steps that overlook the Roman theater and the Adige. Upon reaching the top, your eyes will open wide at the panoramic views of the city. The castle stands before you, and from this vantage point across the Adige, all of Verona lies ceremoniously at your feet, including the cathedral of Santa Maria Maticolare and the church of Sant'Anastasia along the river and the densely built city nestled in its bend.

A castle has stood here on the hill of San Pietro since the short reign of terror of Gian Galeazzo Visconti at the end of the 14th century. Today's building dates from the time of the Austrian occupation.

In the period between 1797 and 1866, Verona was built out as a fortified city, including the strengthening of the city walls, the construction of an enormous arsenal, and the rebuilding of the barracks here at the Castel San Pietro. In the historic brick siege castle were the dormitories for the army and the lodging and offices of the Austrian officers, alongside storerooms and workshops. From its large waterfront hilltop, it was the perfect location from which to control the city, or to bombard it in the case of a battle or revolt. Currently the complex is being renovated for use as a museum.

Address Piazzale Castel San Pietro, 37129 Verona | **Public Transit** Bus 31, 32, 33, 91, 96, 97 to the Teatro Romano stop | **Tip** The restaurant slightly below the castle, TeodoricoRe, invites you to enjoy the magnificent views from its small, peaceful garden.

65__Castelvecchio

Celebrating the architecture of Carlo Scarpa

Cangrande II della Scala commissioned the construction of the Castelvecchio in the middle of the 14th century, including a residential castle on the western portion of the site and a parade ground in the east. In particular, the castle was built to provide protection against possible uprisings of the urban population. In the extreme case, the bridge over the river that was part of the complex offered the possibility of escape. After the end of the Scaligeri reign, the castle remained in military use for centuries. Only in 1924 was it converted into a museum, and its medieval appearance was restored, right up to the battlements.

As in the past, there is only one way into the complex, through the entrance tower on the Corso Castelvecchio, where a drawbridge leads over the ancient moat. What looks like an old palazzo in the inner courtyard is actually a former barracks erected during the French occupation of Verona and later rebuilt in the 1920s for use as a museum, repurposing salvaged windows, loggias, and door frames from destroyed structures around the city. The museum contains a variety of art an artifacts from the Medieval and Romanesque periods.

The garden is a real highlight and it can be explored without buying an admission ticket. It is based on the design of the architect Carlo Scarpa, who was responsible for the renovation of the museum in 1958. Understated rectangular shapes dominate the garden and lawn, with crisscrossing walkways. Near the museum entrance, two fountains splash in shallow pools of water. To the left, you can see into an open system of passageways that interlace the interior of the museum with the outdoors. Even from here, you'll gain an appreciation of Scarpa's typical style, combining local stone materials and traditional plastering techniques with glass, steel beams, and concrete. This juxtaposition is part of the curiosity of this museum, where the presentation is just as interesting as the exhibited art treasures themselves.

Address Corso Castelvecchio 2, 37121 Verona, Tel 0039/045/8062611 | **Public Transit**
Bus 21, 22, 23, 24, 31, 32, 33, 41, 42, 61, 62, 91, 94, 95 to the Corso Castelvecchio
stop | **Hours** Tues–Sun 8:30am–7:30pm, Mon 1:30–7:30pm (ticket office closes at
6:45pm) | **Tip** The design drawings by the architect Carlo Scarpa for the Castelvecchio,
edited by Alba di Lieto, are viewable right here and also in the digital archive found at
www.archiviocarloscarpa.it.

66__ Choir Stalls
Optical illusions in Santa Maria in Organo

The campanile of Santa Maria in Organo is the main landmark of Veronetta, the neighborhood directly across the Adige River from the city center. Once there, the patchy facade of the building is often disappointing to visitors. Michele Sanmicheli's late-16th-century design for a magnificent marble facade for the church was only carried out on the lower half of the building.

The church's greatest treasure can be found inside in the choir. The sacristan who is usually present happily allows visitors in for a closer look and turns on the spotlight. In the bright light, the intricate inlaid wood scenes of the choir come to life. They were created between 1494 and 1499 by the versatile artist Giovanni da Verona, who was also a lay-brother of the Olivetti Convent, located on-site since 1444.

The 27 images on the high backs of the choir stalls never cease to amaze, so artfully composed are the perspective views of differently colored woods. Architectural and landscape scenes alternate with images of cupboards whose half-open doors reveal objects so realistic, you're tempted to reach in and grab them. Most of the cupboards contain two shelves filled front to back with books, liturgical and astronomical equipment, candelabras, clocks, flowers in vases, and other objects. The artist skillfully used space and the play between shadow and light in all the scenes, especially the vedute – i.e., those depicting the cityscape.

In one inlay, Fra Giovanni da Verona portrays the church of Santa Maria in Organo with a completed campanile, showing its original design. The church didn't complete the bell tower until 1553, and the final construction differs slightly from that depicted by the artist. In the adjacent sacristy, similar cabinets were created at a later point, where the spectrum of themes of the wood inlay is again varied. A large barn owl and the Arena of Verona appear deceptively real.

Address Piazzetta Santa Maria in Organo, 37129 Verona | **Public Transit** Bus 31, 32, 33, 73, 91, 96, 97 to the Piazza Isolo stop | **Hours** Generally open daily | **Tip** It is worth a visit to the palazzo housing the Bishop's Seminary, where a loggia on the upper floors features a fresco from 1789 that depicts the heavens, including personifications of the constellations.

67 __ The Christmas Market
The tradition of Santa Lucia

In Verona and certain other areas around the Lake Garda region, it isn't Saint Nicholas who brings candy and gifts to children at Christmastime, but rather Saint Lucy, known in these parts as Santa Lucia.

On December 12th, every child sets out their shoes or a small plate. Milk and cookies are prepared for Santa Lucia and her helper Gastaldo, and a carrot and water are left for the donkey who pulls their heavy cart. The next morning, the snacks are gone and the shoes or plate are full of presents and treats. If a child isn't well-behaved over the course of the year, it is said he or she will find coal in place of the gifts – an occurrence about as frequent as its American counterpart.

Reverence of Santa Lucia, who died during the persecution of Christians in the 4th century A.D., has a long tradition in Verona. It was a miracle, though, that truly established her popularity among the people. During the 18th century, a terrible epidemic left many children in the city blind. Parents and the afflicted went barefoot in a procession to what was then the Church of Lucia. The church was regarded for its "holy light and eyes" due to the Latin roots of Lucy's name, *lux*, which means "light." The epidemic came to an end soon after the procession, and in gratitude to the saint, the townspeople made it an annual event. If the children marched with bare feet, they could expect to find a surprise in their shoes when they returned home.

This tradition also gave rise to the Verona Christmas Market, the Mercatino di Santa Lucia, held each year from December 10th to 13th. More than 300 stalls fill the Piazza Bra, offering all sorts of craft items and delicacies, such as the Pastefrolle di Santa Lucia pastries. The picturesque scene is capped with a huge sculpture of an illuminated shooting star whose tail arcs out of the square and ends gracefully in the Roman Arena.

Address Piazza Bra, 37121 Verona | **Public Transit** Bus 11, 12, 13, 72, 90, 92, 93, 96, 97, 98, 510 to the Piazza Bra stop | **Hours** Dec 10–12 9:30am–11pm, Dec 13 9:30am–8pm | **Tip** Walking down the festively decorated Via Mazzini will lead you to the Piazza delle Erbe and its Christmas tree, illuminated beautifully by countless tiny lights.

68__Colonna di San Marco

Catching up with friends and La Serenissima

The tall pillar topped with a lion springs to life on warm evenings. It seems as though half of Verona comes here on the weekends to hang out with friends and grab an aperitif, a glass of wine, or a beer. As late as midnight, the northern end of the Piazza delle Erbe is so full of young people and the noise level so high that you can barely understand a single word. The bars around the piazza, in particular the Bar Casa Mazzanti, provide refreshments that help keep the revelry lively.

Ask anyone in Verona, and they'll be able to tell you the history of the column. Beginning in 1405, the city came under the rule of the Venetian Republic for almost 300 years. La Serenissima, as Venice was known, cleverly and carefully balanced securing the peace within their territory while at the same time allowing the city of Verona considerable freedom. Their continuous reign was only interrupted for eight years, from 1509 to 1517, when Maximilian I, emperor of the Holy Roman Empire, occupied the city. On March 15, 1524, it is said that the city of Verona itself erected the Colonna di San Marco to express their devotion to Venice after this brief interlude.

The inscription on the pedestal of the column gives the year of its completion and names Michele Leoni as the head architect. The smooth, white marble column concludes with a capital displaying four coats of arms, namely that of Verona, of then ruling Doge Andrea Gritti, and of the two overarching Venetian government officials, the *podestà* and the *capitano*. Including the winged lion of Saint Mark enthroned atop, the towering structure reaches a height of nearly forty feet.

The column was a thorn in the side of the Napoleonic troops who invaded Verona in 1797. Rather than tearing it down completely, however, they only destroyed the symbol of the old rulers, which was then restored by the Veronese in 1886.

Address Piazza delle Erbe, 37121 Verona | **Public Transit** Bus 70 to the Piazza Erbe stop; Bus 96, 97 to the Lungadige Rubele stop | **Tip** In the middle of the square stands the 16th-century *berlina*, a marble canopy that originally included a bench, where the city's leading officials, such as the *podestà*, were publicly introduced.

69_ Corte Sgarzarie

Outdoor dining at the old cloth guildhall

A decorated roundabout archway in the facade of the house at number 14 Corso Porta Borsari can't help but arouse your curiosity. It leads into a passageway through the building, but it's clear that it's open to the public and not a private corridor. The inscription on a tablet above the arch informs us that in this area were based the wool weavers, who were the economic lifeblood of Verona from the 14th to the 15th century, and for whom the city was famous throughout Europe.

A two-story loggia extends along the right side of the entrance to the Corte Sgarzarie. It so completely fills the courtyard that narrow paths provide the only access to the surrounding rows of houses. Though nowadays this is a somewhat sleepy corner of the city, this old commercial center of the wool-processing industry once hummed with activity. The loggia, which was probably constructed in the middle of the 14th century, served as the market hall for the bustling cloth trade. In the open-air structure below, the fine wool fabrics were measured, weighed, and marked with the official stamps needed for trade. The enclosed rooms above were used for storage.

Sgarzarie is a term from the Veronese dialect used for the workshops of the *garzatori* that lined the courtyard. These were the people responsible for the final step in the cloth-production process, namely the roughening of the felted wool fabrics. Before it reached them, the lambswool was washed and purified on the banks of the Adige River, then spun and woven into cloth, and finally processed in the fulling mills.

Today the open floor of the loggia is used by the surrounding bars for outdoor seating and the rooms above are used as offices. Hardly anyone seems to remember that this building was once the financial heart of the city and that the valuable goods produced here were traded all over Europe.

Address Corte Sgarzarie, 37121 Verona | **Public Transit** Bus 70 to the Piazza Erbe stop; Bus 96, 97 to the Lungadige Rubele stop | **Tip** Across the Corso Porta Borsari from the hall down the winding Vicolo San Marco in Foro lies the Palazzo Lonardi, whose facade is decorated with frescoes from the early 16th century by Giovanni Maria Falconetto.

70_ Dante Alighieri
The Italian poet on the Piazza dei Signori

The Piazza dei Signori never had a true focal point until 1865, when a statue of Dante Alighieri was placed in its center. With that it also received its informal second name, the Piazza Dante. A highly recommended restaurant facing the square is also named after the greatest poet and philosopher of the Italian Middle Ages: Antico Caffè Dante.

Dante Alighieri (1265–1321) looms larger than life atop a high pedestal, elevated above the action on the piazza. The white marble sculpture depicts him standing in the pose of a thinker, pensive as he holds the index finger of his right hand to his chin. A stack of papers hangs from the fingers of his left hand, suggesting that the poet is contemplating one of his writings. His distinctive facial features – particular his hooked nose – are known by many thanks to the pictures of his supposed death mask, and by a whole new generation from the back of the Italian two-euro coin. He also wears the typical male headgear of the time, a linen cap with long lappets over the ears.

The statue, created by the sculptor Ugo Zannoni, was installed on May 14, 1865, six hundred years after his presumed birthday, as it says in the inscription on its base. It also points out that Dante first took refuge in Verona during his exile, which the sculpture is meant to commemorate.

Dante, who held public office in his hometown of Florence and was caught up in political feuds, is believed to have first sought assistance from Bartolomeo della Scala here in Verona in 1304. Between 1312 and 1318, he was said to have returned to Verona while working on various writings, the *Paradiso* portion of the *Divine Comedy* being the most important. This he dedicated to the man who, he felt, possessed the ideal personality for a ruler: Cangrande I della Scala, who once resided in the Palazzo at the head of the very same Piazza dei Signori.

Address Piazza dei Signori, 37121 Verona | **Public Transit** Bus 70 to the Piazza Erbe stop; Bus 96, 97 to the Lungadige Rubele stop | **Tip** In 1320, Dante presented his famous cosmological work, *Quaestio di acqua e terra*, in the small church of Sant'Elena (within the cathedral complex).

71 Denunciation Mailboxes
Telling secrets in the Piazza dei Signori

What would happen in this country to mailboxes that have not been used for more than two hundred years? The answer seems immediately obvious, but the same cannot be said for Italy. Here, historic buildings have remained intact down to the smallest details, some of which are quite fascinating. Of particular interest are three mailboxes still attached to the exterior walls of public buildings in Verona, dating back to the time of Venetian rule.

These "mailboxes" took the form of grotesque faces, or *bocche*, which were attached to the walls of these buildings along with marble panels bearing inscriptions announcing their purpose. Into their contorted mouths, anonymous letters could be stuck by anyone secretly denouncing lawbreakers to the authorities for usury and other such crimes.

The first of these so-called *bocche per le denunzie* can be seen on the facade of the Palazzo della Ragione facing the Piazza dei Signori, once the political and administrative hub of Verona. During Venetian times, starting in 1405, this former city hall building housed the local tax authorities. Just to the left of the entrance, a plaque reads: *denunzie secret. contro usurarj e contrati usuratici di qualunque sorte.* Any usurer and anyone guilty of usury could be secretly revealed here through an unsigned note.

The second *bocca* lies somewhat hidden on the side of the very same building, around the corner in the alleyway. It was meant specifically to identify and accuse any smugglers who threatened the Venetian monopoly on silk.

The third mailbox is located in the courtyard of the building immediately to the south, the Palazzo del Capitano. This building served as the seat of the Venetian *capitano*, who was responsible for the safety and military security of the city. Right next to the Porta dei Bombardieri is a fearsome lion whose mouth was the repository for accusations of gunpowder smuggling.

DENUNZIE SECRET.^E
CONTRO USURARJ,
E CONTRATI
USURATICI DI
QUALUNQUE SORTE.

Address Piazza dei Signori, 37121 Verona | **Public Transit** Bus 70 to the Piazza Erbe stop; Bus 96, 97 to the Lungadige Rubele stop | **Tip** The outdoor terraces of the three restaurants in the piazza are a great way to appreciate the beautiful square and the details of its surrounding buildings.

72__Giardino Giusti

A garden paradise with a menacing mask

A visit to the Giardino Giusti on the eastern edge of the old city is a must for any visitor to Verona, particularly for those seeking a bit of tranquility and calm. Even from the street, a look through the arched entryway of the Renaissance palace offers a view up the main cypress-lined path of the garden. This walkway leads up to a cave and continues to the *mascherone* at the garden's highest point. This huge grotesque mask carved into the rock once shot tongues of fire out of its gaping mouth on festival days.

Starting in the 1570s, Agostino Giusti, cavaliere of the Republic of Venice and nobleman of the Grand Duchy of Tuscany, commissioned the magnificent garden, which in large part retains its original form. The palace and park are still owned by the Giusti family, who maintain its excellent condition and make it accessible to the public for a small fee.

Near the entrance to the gardens, hedges are laid out in geometric patterns interspersed with statues and fountains. These artistic pieces, together with the landscaping, signal that this area was originally conceived of as a garden museum. Continuing along the path, you are embraced by the sound of birdsong and the scent of the blooming lemon trees.

Farther up the hill, the view starts to change as you enter a cool and refreshing forest area. The pathway ends at a small tower with a winding staircase that climbs over the rock wall to a belvedere. As its name suggests, it offers a marvelous panoramic view over the entire city.

Among the many famous visitors to the Giardino Giusti was Johann Wolfgang Goethe, to whom an old cypress at the entrance to the pathway is dedicated. During his 1786 tour through the gardens, he admired the setting quite a bit, remarking: "A tree, whose branches … aspire to heaven, a feat that takes some three hundred years, is well worth our worship."

Address Via Giardino Giusti 2, 37121 Verona | **Public Transit** Bus 31, 32, 33, 91 to the Via Giusti stop; Bus 72 to the Via Sauro stop | **Hours** Apr–Sep, daily 9am–8pm; Oct–Mar, daily 9am–7pm | **Tip** On the return trip to the city center, veer off of the Via Carducci and explore its many small side streets, where the character of old city is well preserved.

73_ The Ginkgo Trees

Fine specimens on the Piazza Indipendenza

There aren't many lush public parks found within the city center of Verona. While there are a handful of green spaces scattered about, like that of the Piazza Bra and those found on various street corners, they are typically not properly cared for. One would think, then, that when the temperatures rise, parents and grandparents with their small children in tow would make their way to the leafy manicured park at the Piazza Indipendenza. But no, they'd rather meet for their afternoon get-togethers just steps away, in the Piazza dei Signori, where they sit on the shaded steps of the Palazzo del Consiglio while their children spin their wheels on the smooth flagstones of the square.

Some years ago, the city council began discussing a project to build an underground parking lot beneath the Piazza Indipendenza in the former Palazzo delle Poste, and an outcry rang out among the population. People were concerned for the safety and preservation of the old trees that dot the piazza – which was the city's botanical gardens during the Scaligeri era – especially two tall ginkgos. Their petition was successful, and in 2012, the design for the project was revised in order to save the trees.

The pair of ginkgos are indeed impressive. Their thick trunks stand so close together that they form a common treetop with a height of over 80 feet. They stand at the outer northwestern corner of the high-lying park, so their branches reach well above the adjacent streets and can be seen from all around. Experts estimate them to be more than 200 years old, placing them among the earliest ginkgo specimens on Italian soil.

Since the trees were threatened, the people of Verona have rekindled their appreciation of the lovely park and now frequently enjoy themselves in the shade of the bright green fan-shaped leaves of the towering gingkos, savoring the golden light created by their yellow color in the fall.

Address Piazza Indipendenza, 37121 Verona | **Public Transit** Bus 70 to the Piazza Viviani stop; Bus 96, 97 to the Lungadige Rubele stop | **Tip** In the Teatro Nuovo, a neoclassical building on the neighboring Piazza Francesco Viviani, theater performances are staged all year long.

74__Girolamo Fracastoro
Quite an auspicious statue

The Piazza dei Signori has always been the political center of Verona. Though the many public buildings that surround the square date from different periods, city planners used a trick to lend the piazza an overall harmony. All of the various pathways branching off from the piazza are spanned by archways that link all the buildings together.

While some of these archways actually function as passageways between two buildings, others serve only to connect them visually, like the arch over the Via delle Fogge. It was constructed in 1492 to span from the Loggia del Consiglio, the imposing municipal building, over to the renovated facade of a building formerly known as the Casa di Pietà. In 1559, a statue of Girolamo Fracastoro, created by the sculptor Danese Cattaneo, was placed atop it.

The Loggia del Consiglio was already crowned with a set of five sculptures representing ancient Veronese personalities such as Catullus and Pliny the Elder. The statue of Fracastoro brought the series forward into the present. The famous astronomer, physician, and poet, who spent his entire life in Verona, had been dead for only two years when the city council decided to build this statue in his honor. His facial features and long beard correspond with contemporary portraits of him, but his toga gives him the air of being a much older, ancient philosopher.

In his right hand Fracastoro holds a large ball, representing the world. This *bala de Fracastoro*, as the ball was baptized in dialect, is connected to a prophecy: *Cadrà sulla testa del primo galantuomo che passerà sotto* – that is, it will fall on top of the first gentleman who passes under the arch. Originally meant as a mocking allusion to the judges and lawyers who used this walkway to reach the courthouse, the saying lives on today, and you can now wait for the ball to point out your ever elusive Mr. Right. Needless to say, Fracastoro has never dropped the ball.

HIER· FRACASTORIO
PAVLLI PHILIPPI· F·
EX PVBLICA AVCToRITATE
DICATA
AN· SAL· M·D·LIX

Address Piazza dei Signori / Via delle Fogge, 37121 Verona | **Public Transit** Bus 70 to the Piazza Erbe stop; Bus 96, 97 to the Lungadige Rubele stop | **Tip** Statues were later placed atop other arches between the buildings of the Piazza dei Signori, such as that of Scipione Maffei over the Volto Barbaro in 1756.

75__ The Holy Water Fonts

Sights to behold in the church of Sant'Anastasia

Sant'Anastasia is the largest church in Verona. It lies at the head of the Corso and already comes into view from the Porta Borsari. The Dominicans began construction on the building in 1290, and it was consecrated in 1471. Today, the facade of the sacred building still remains unfinished.

The massive construction project brought several donors and benefactors to the brink of bankruptcy. Until the 14th century, the ruling della Scala family and the nobleman Guglielmo di Castelbarco counted among the major sponsors of the church. After a long interruption, work was resumed in the 15th century and in the end was guided only by the joint financial efforts of the Catholic Church, the city, and its citizens.

Two holy water fonts – which immediately catch your eye as you enter the church – seem to allude to the fact that the people of Verona felt brought to their knees by the massive undertaking. On the left side of the entryway, a man clad in a simple shirt and bare feet sits on the pedestal of the first column. His contorted face makes clear that he is hardly able to support the weight that rests on his back. The overhanging and richly decorated holy water font is surely to be understood as *pars pro toto* for the church.

The marble sculpture is attributed to the sculptor Gabriele Caliari, father of the famous painter Paolo Veronese. He is said to have created this *Gobbo*, or hunchback, in 1495. Its counterpart can be found opposite, on the right side with the *Pasquino* – so called because this font and support were installed on Easter in 1591 (*Pasqua* is Italian for "Easter").

The pair of sculptures are now considered great works of art, and their tone has since taken on a positive note. It is believed even today that whomever touches the hump of the *Gobbo* will be the recipient of good luck – and may even be capable of such an incredible feat as his.

Address Piazza Sant'Anastasia, 37121 Verona | Public Transit Bus 70, 96, 97 to the Via Massalongo stop | Hours Mon–Sat 9:30am–6pm, Sun 1–6pm | Tip The Arca di Castelbarco, the memorial monument to the great sponsor of Sant'Anastasia, runs from the left facade of the church back to the small church of San Giorgetto.

76__Istituto Don Calabria

Headquarters of the worldwide religious order

On the terrace of the Istituto Don Calabria (Don Calabria Institute), far above the humming of the busy city, you feel like you are outside the realm of space and time. Visitors can easily lose themselves in the huge expanse of the grounds, walking among the long shadows. The gigantic, brightly colored building complex that houses the religious social institution is built into the hillside along the Adige River, and resembles a self-sufficient oasis.

Giovanni Calabria is counted among the great personalities of Verona. The priest and founder of the order, who was beatified in 1988 and canonized in 1999 by Pope John Paul II, was born in 1873 in Verona. Following his father's untimely death, Calabria, the son of a poor family with many children, was given the possibility of a formal education through the support of a priest who helped him gain entrance into seminary school.

From the very beginning of his theological studies Calabria showed his propensity for good deeds by taking care of a homeless gypsy child he found on the street. His mercy and tireless commitment to the socially and economically disadvantaged led him in 1908 to set up what's known today as the Istituto Casa Buoni Fanciulli, a kind of youth village where poor and sick children can receive an education and technical training.

The complex, located in an elevated position at the edge of the city, had been built as a monastery, but was secularized by the French and then used by the Austrians as barracks. A nobleman donated the buildings for use by the institute. Today only the small church of San Zeno in Monte remains from the old monastery, where Don Calabria, who died on December 4th, 1954, is buried. The institute was expanded in 1936, its design echoing back extensively to the historic structure. As before, it is the headquarters of the Congregation of the Poor Servants of Divine Providence, currently operating around the world.

Address Via San Zeno in Monte, 37129 Verona | **Public Transit** Bus 31, 32, 33, 91 to the Via Giardino Giusti stop, Bus 72 to the Via Sauro stop | **Hours** Generally open daily | **Tip** From the Via Scala Santa, you can reach the Romanesque church of San Giovanni in Valle, with its crypt dating from the 10th century.

77 __ The Juliet Statue

A stand-in for the star-crossed lover

Picturing a story in your head is significantly easier if specific suggestions are made to stimulate the imagination. This could be what went through the mind of the director of the museums of Verona in 1935 when he chose to install a medieval tomb as a balcony at the Casa di Giulietta, or house of Juliet, the alleged home of the Capulets. Since then, visitors have imagined that this is where Juliet must have stood when speaking to her true love below, and where Romeo climbed up into her bedroom on their wedding night. The truth is that Shakespeare never mentions a balcony in the story; he only writes of a window. What he also wrote about is the golden image of Juliet. At the end of the tragedy, Romeo's father declares: "… For I will raise her statue in pure gold."

In 1972, the local Lions Club made a gift of a gilded bronze sculpture of Juliet, which was placed in the cortile of the house. She stands almost life-size, seemingly lost in thought, her left hand upon her chest – or more accurately – over her heart, while her right hand grasps at her long robe, lifting it slightly into folds. Nereo Costantini had completed the sculpture three years earlier, using as his model a particularly beautiful young woman from the aristocracy of Verona, Luisa Braguzzi, the wife of Conte Eugenio Morando di Custoza.

The guards have difficulty monitoring and managing the passageway to the inner courtyard, where visitors paste notes to the wall and draw little hearts inscribed with their initials. They clean the walls repeatedly to allow subsequent visitors their own turn. One task they never have to worry about is polishing the statue. It is kept shiny by the innumerable visitors who pose with it for a photo, and by those who believe that copping a quick feel will bring luck in love. So Juliet remains pure glistening gold, and our identification with her love story seems to assume ever more incredible dimensions.

Address Via Cappello 23, 37121 Verona | **Public Transit** Bus 70 to the Piazza Erbe stop; Bus 96, 97 to the Lungadige Rubele stop | **Hours** Mon 1:30–7:30pm, Tues–Sun 8:30am–7:30pm | **Tip** The Casa di Giulietta, with its beautiful historic rooms, is furnished as a museum. The opening hours are the same as those of the inner courtyard (ticket office closes at 6:45pm).

78__Juliet's Tomb

Recreating a memorable Hollywood moment

There are plenty of signs to help you find your way to the former Capuchin monastery of San Francesco al Corso housing the Tomba di Giulietta (tomb of Juliet). Because its location is somewhat outside of the city center, however, the 14th-century cloister is far from being a pilgrimage place like the busy Casa di Giulietta on Via Cappello.

In both cases, it was the idea of the director of the Museums of Verona, Antonio Avena, to boost tourism by concretely locating the scenes from Shakespeare's famous play in actual places. An antique red marble sarcophagus had probably stood around in the monastery's garden for centuries when Avena came upon it. In 1937, he created an imaginary backstory for the *tomba* and had it set up in an arched vault of the cloister. The film version of *Romeo and Juliet*, a dramatic 1936 production of Metro-Goldwyn-Mayer, had probably tipped the balance in favor of the sarcophagus's new home. The film was not shot in Verona, but the pivotal scene showing the death of the lovers, played by Leslie Howard and Norma Shearer, was set in a crypt. In order not to disappoint tourists, who planned their visit to Verona as a result of the Oscar-nominated blockbuster, the lidless coffin was presented in a similar spatial context.

The Museo degli Affreschi ("museum of frescoes") has been housed in the monastery since 1973. Approximately 50 frescoes from facades and interiors of destroyed buildings from around the city are on display here. The most beautiful hall is equipped with frescoes taken in 1970 from the loggia of the Palazzo Guarienti. Between 1560 and 1570, Paolo Farinati painted several allegorical figures and mythological scenes framed by false columns. Civil weddings have been performed in this hall for some time, and newlyweds can now imagine themselves in the presence of the eternally perfect couple Romeo and Juliet, who remained together till death did they part.

Address Museo degli Affreschi G.B. Cavalcaselle, Via del Pontiere 35, 37121 Verona, Tel. 0039/045/8000361 | **Public Transit** Bus 51, 73 to the Via Montanari stop | **Hours** Tues–Sun 8:30am–7:30pm, Mon 1:45–7:30pm (ticket office closes at 6:45pm) | **Tip** A stroll over the recently remodeled Piazza Cittadella leads back to the Piazza Bra.

79__Lion Figures

How the Porta dei Leoni got its name

Figures of lions feature prominently around Verona: two marble lions support the porches on the main facade of both the Cathedral and the Basilica of San Zeno Maggiore, and they are seen in symbols of the city's former Venetian rulers at the Piazza delle Erbe and Piazza dei Signori.

So, given that its name means "gate of the lions," you would naturally expect to find representations of lions on the Roman Porta dei Leoni, too. Your assumption would be incorrect, however, because the gate on the Via Cappello only received its current name in the 16th century. People were excited by the nearby discovery of a Roman sarcophagus, the lid of which was decorated with two lions. The enthusiasm for these artistic representations from antiquity was apparently so great that henceforth, the gate was referred to as the Porta dei Leoni.

The city gate would have been adorned in the first century A.D. with a grand facade of white marble, but today only half of the structure remains intact and it is built into the side of a house. It originally lined the Cardus Maximus, the busy Roman thoroughfare traced today by the Via Cappello. An excavation area going down about six feet, viewable from the road that passes on both sides, shows that the gate was originally connected to a massive reinforced fortress with towers.

If you follow the line of the street farther in the direction of the Adige River, a statue comes into view on the patch of grass before the Ponte delle Navi. The inscription on its base identifies the man with his characteristic mustache as Umberto I, king of Italy from 1878 to 1900. The pedestal is framed by two thick olive trees, and barely noticeable behind them is the very Roman relic that gave the Porta dei Leoni its name. The marble plate with its two lions lying horizontally, their heads stretched toward the viewer, sits amid the grass, nearly forgotten.

Address Corner of Via Leoni and Lungadige Rubele, 37121 Verona | **Public Transit** Bus 11, 12, 13, 51, 73, 90, 92, 98, 510 to the San Fermo stop | **Tip** On the Ponte delle Navi, couples hang "love locks" similar to those on the Pont des Arts in Paris and the Ponte Milvio in Rome.

80 __ Liston 12

The place to be seen on the Piazza Bra

To refer to the Liston as merely a sidewalk would be a gross understatement. If you asked an Italian for his opinion, he would probably say, "*Liston è Liston*," just as the old advertisement proclaimed that "Ferrari is Ferrari." The Liston is simply unique, and not just by Veronese standards. Its broad surface extends between Via Roma and Via Mazzini (the most elegant shopping street in the city) on the Piazza Bra.

The Liston is lined with three-story palazzi with bars and restaurants on the ground floors. Their outdoor terraces occupy a large sweeping footprint on the piazza, but there is still plenty of room for a promenade. The Veronese stroll over here dressed to the nines in the evening and on Sundays to see and be seen. In the popular bar Liston 12, which uses its address as its name, you can watch the wonderful action over a *caffè* or *aperitivo*.

The Liston is part of the Piazza Bra, the spacious square surrounding the Arena di Verona, which only gained importance in the context of the city in 1530, when the Porta Nuova was built and a direct connection between it and the main thoroughfare, the Corso Porta Nuova, was created.

As a result, a flurry of construction activity began on the palazzi along its western edge, including the stately home built in 1555 by Veronese architect Michele Sanmicheli for the degli Honorij merchant family. The architect had already hinted at the Roman architecture of the Arena in his design for the imposing city gate, but he produced a direct reflection of it in the arcade of the palazzo, with its rough ashlar masonry.

On the southern side of the square, the large buildings of the Palazzo della Gran Guardia and the Palazzo Barbieri – the current seat of the local government – were built in the 18th and 19th centuries. The surface of the Piazza Bra is nonetheless dominated by the Liston, paved in 1770 with large slabs of Veronese marble.

Address Piazza Bra 12, 37121 Verona | **Public Transit** Bus 11, 12, 13, 72, 90, 92, 93, 96, 97, 98, 510 to the Piazza Bra stop | **Hours** Mon–Sun 7:30am–2 or 3am (during the opera season it also stays open after performances); in the winter months, Mon–Sun 7:30am–11pm or midnight | **Tip** Near the start of the Via Mazzini is a column topped by an aedicula, dating from about 1350, with statues of Mary and three saints in a Gothic portico.

81 Lo Spino del Filo Spinato

The sculpture on the Piazza Isolo

This sculpture is the focal point of the Piazza Isolo and provides a level of scale to the hard form and large expanse of the surrounding square. The wide space was at one time an island between the Adige River and a small tributary, which was drained and backfilled in 1882. The square was redesigned in 2001 in conjunction with the construction of an underground parking garage. After work was completed in 2009, the sculpture *Lo Spino del Filo Spinato* (The Sting of the Barbed Wire) found its place here.

The monumental bronze work literally explodes out of the stone pavement, and the bright slabs of marble that cover the piazza are blown aside by its dynamism. Two of the plates bear inscriptions that explain the meaning and background of the sculpture. It is dedicated to the victims of World War II, particularly the Jews who died in the concentration camps. Pino Castagna created the work on behalf of a committee of citizens of Verona and with the support of the Banca Popolare di Verona and the Cariverona Foundation.

The Lake Garda-based sculptor chose barbed wire as the subject for his piece to symbolize exclusion and oppression. Giant arms extend out equally in all directions from the central mass of twisted wire, and the sculpture reaches 23 feet in both height and width.

Upon closer inspection of the work, another message surfaces. The arms don't end in points as they would normally do with barbed wire, but rather grow wider as they extend out from the center. In this respect, the central node has the effect of a bundle of energy that radiates out into the environment. This momentum seems to suggest an act of liberation and in so doing appeals to its viewers: If our general awareness is sharpened, the tragedies of the past will not be repeated. So Pino Castagna calls upon us with his sculpture to *ricordare per non dimenticare*: to "remember by not forgetting."

Address Piazza Isolo, 37121 Verona | Public Transit Bus 31, 32, 33, 73, 91, 96, 97 to the Piazza Isolo stop | Tip On the corner of Interrato Dell'Aqua Morta and Lungadige Teodorico stands a memorial to the famous painter Paolo Veronese, who was named after his hometown.

82 Madonna and Child

A devotional image on the Via Sottoriva

Tranquility reigns over the picturesque Via Sottoriva. The colorful buildings on the west side of the street are connected to one another by a long, deep arched portico decked by high exposed wood beam ceilings. The restaurants housed in these buildings offer shaded outdoor seating under the archways, providing relief on hot summer days.

The name of the street explains its topography: *sottoriva* means "below the bank" in Italian, and the street is located beneath the level of the Adige River. Because of this, the neighborhood was often flooded when the river rose, and it was particularly affected by the flood of 1882, which wiped out hundreds of buildings throughout Verona and much of the town's industry – its watermills and sawmills – and wrecked the two main bridges. As a result, new walls and massive bank fortifications were constructed to control the river and protect the surrounding areas.

An ethereal light catches your eye under the shaded portico of Via Sottoriva. It illuminates a devotional image of Mary with the infant Jesus. The Baroque enclosure turns the fresco in its wooden frame into a small altar. From above, the eye of God and a number of cherubs watch over the Madonna. The white lace doily on the altar plate and the flowers regularly placed atop it are testament to how carefully this revered image is maintained.

The devotional painting, which probably dates from the 18th century, is considered miraculous by believers because it survived the flood in 1882, after which Cardinal Luigi di Canossa, the bishop of Verona since 1861, had a marble plaque installed on the front of the house. It says that anyone who prays the *Ave Maria*, or Hail Mary, in front of the image is granted an indulgence for 100 days.

Today the pious still pray before the small veiled altar, and a rosary is prayed every Thursday evening at around 9pm during the Marian month of May.

83 _Madonna Verona

The quirky symbol of the city

The people of Verona love the *Madonna Verona*, the personification of their city, and on warm summer days they enjoy the soothing murmur of the fountain sculpture standing in the middle of the Piazza delle Erbe.

Cansignorio, the last of the powerful Scaligeri rulers, commissioned the building of the fountain in 1368. If you look closely at the central figure though, a few incongruities will strike you as odd, most notably that the rounded head does not quite fit on the elaborate marble body clad in flowing robes. You're not seeing things: Cansignorio had pieces from different ancient statues molded together to create a whole new figure. The damaged statue of an ancient goddess, most likely found on the site of the Roman-era Forum, was reincarnated with the addition of a head and arms taken from other statues. A crown fashioned from a sheet of copper was placed atop her head and in her hands she holds a ribbon that reads: *est justi latrix urbs haec et laudis amatrix* ("This city is the bearer of justice and the lover of praise").

The huge red marble basin of the fountain is also an ancient relic. The column, which rises from the basin and supports the statue, is decorated with two rows of crowned heads whose mouths spew jets of water into the basin. Water overflows the slanted central platform and collects in a large round trough. One of the crowned heads on the column is inscribed *(mar)morea verona* and symbolizes Queen Verona a second time.

Cansignorio sought to make a statement with the piece and presented it as his contribution to the common good. In continuity with the ancients, he designed Verona as a "city of marble" and adorned it with this fountain.

The *Fontana di Madonna Verona* is fed from a water pipe, which was renewed during Cansignorios' reign. It led the springwater of the river Lorì here from Avesa, to the north.

Address Piazza delle Erbe, 37121 Verona | **Public Transit** Bus 70 to the Piazza Erbe stop; Bus 96, 97 to the Lungadige Rubele stop | **Tip** There are a handful of stalls on the Piazza delle Erbe selling delicious, freshly prepared *macedonia*, or fruit salad.

84 Michele Sanmicheli

The tomb of the celebrated Renaissance architect

Michele Sanmicheli is counted among the greatest sons of Verona. The scion of a famous family of sculptors and artists, he was born in Verona in 1487 or 1488 and was the architect responsible for giving the city its distinctive character. Unlike Palladio in Vicenza or Giulio Romano in Mantua, Sanmicheli not only designed private buildings and churches, but also worked as an engineer on the building of the city walls for the Republic of Venice and was entrusted with the modernization of the fortifications and their associated urban development measures. In his design of palaces, churches, or city gates, he recalled the ancient architecture of Verona. Some of the most notable examples of his work include the Pellegrini Chapel, the Palazzo Pompei (see page 182), the Porta Nuova, and the Porta Palio (see page 202).

After his death, in 1559, Sanmicheli was buried in the church of San Tomaso Cantuariense, the parish near his home to which he had belonged throughout his life. His original marble gravestone can still be seen there, along with the neoclassical monument that was built in 1886 following a revival in the appreciation of his work. In the single-nave church it is located behind the entrance on the wall to the right.

The white Carrara marble bust simply glows in its architectural frame, which is made from various colors of Veronese marble. The bust was created from an engraving made of the High Renaissance architect during his lifetime, and depicts him as an old man with a long beard and dignified expression. In the central field of the pedestal is a carving of a compass and set square, representing the typical instruments of a planning architect. Today, small seating arrangements with art supplies are set up for young children underneath the sculpture to keep them occupied during mass. In this way, the little ones can practice drawing here under the tutelage of the great master.

Address Stradone San Tomaso 1, 37129 Verona | **Public Transit** Bus 72 to the Via Carducci stop | **Hours** Generally open daily | **Tip** In 1769, then 13-year-old Wolfgang Amadeus Mozart gave an organ concert here and carved his initials (WSM, for Wolfgang Salisburgensis Mozart) with a pocketknife in the wooden organ bench.

85 Mille Miglia

A sight to behold, not just for racing fans

You don't have to be a car enthusiast to get excited about the Mille Miglia. The legendary classic car race is held annually each May and its long route is lined by throngs of wildly cheering and clapping spectators.

The focus of the race these days isn't on speed, however, but on uniform, skillful driving, since the cars participating are all antique treasures. Only models of vehicles already in existence during the first iteration of the Mille Miglia, between 1927 and 1957, may participate, a rule that was put in place when the event was revived back in 1977.

The Mille Miglia, which means "thousand-mile," runs over three days on a circuit course of public roads from Brescia through Ferrara to Rome and back again, traversing six regions and some of the most beautiful cities of Italy. The starting flag is waved after the nearly 400 participating classic cars have presented themselves to the crowds in the center of Brescia and passed their technical inspections. During the first stage, the race passes through several towns along Lake Garda on its way to Verona, including Desenzano, Sirmione, and Peschiera del Garda.

Upon arrival in Verona, participants are greeted with a grand reception. The classic autos are driven over the Ponte Scaligero, the bridge over the Adige connected to the Castelvecchio – which is normally open only to pedestrians and cyclists.

On their zigzagging course through the city, you can admire the decked-out sports cars in action, including models from Alfa Romeo, Ferrari, Aston Martin, BMW, and Mercedes. Drivers and passengers in convertibles wear authentic racing caps and goggles. They curve around the Piazza delle Erbe and obtain a stamp of inspection during a quick stop at the Arena, and later that night continue on to Vicenza, Padua, Rovigo, and finally up to Ferrara, the finish line of the race's first stage.

Address Ponte Scaligero, 37121 Verona | **Public Transit** Bus 21, 22, 23, 24, 31, 32, 33, 41, 42, 61, 62, 91, 94, 95 to the Corso Castelvecchio stop | **Hours** Three days in May. Information about the specific dates can be found at www.1000miglia.eu. On the first day of the race, the cars gather in Verona at 8:30pm. | **Tip** Grab a snack or a glass of wine at one of the many bars lining the course, where you can watch the action as it passes by.

86 Museo Maffeiano

One of the first public museums in Europe

In 1745, at the initiative of the Marchese Scipione Maffei, a permanent public exhibition of objects found on archaeological digs around the region was set up here at the Museo Lapidario Maffeiano, directly adjacent to the Portoni della Bra. The museum's entrance, however, can be difficult for the public to find, as the building is surrounded by a huge arcade.

Scipione Maffei was a member of the Accademia Filarmonica, a society of Veronese writers, scientists, and philosophers founded in the 16th century. The Accademia quickly developed into a center of cultural life in Verona and organized concerts, festivals, and theater performances.

In 1605, the group commissioned the design of a theater near the Portoni della Bra by the architect Domenico Curtoni, a student of the famous architect Palladio. It remained unfinished, however, up to the portico with its six monumental Ionic columns. Maffei set about not only completing the construction of the theater, but also establishing in its courtyard a *museo lapidario*, or museum dedicated to stones and gems. He gathered numerous ancient artifacts and inscribed stones within the building's walls. The Republic of Venice supported the museum concept and allowed all of the archaeological finds from the city and surrounding areas to be merged together here.

The idea of a concentrated exhibit of artistic objects from antiquity seems to have gone to Maffei's head, however, and he also sought unsuccessfully to have the massive Porta dei Leoni and the enormous porphyry basin from the Basilica of San Zeno Maggiore installed in the courtyard. Regardless, the existing collection of reliefs, urns, sarcophagi, gravestones and sculptures – presented in the buildings on the Portoni della Bra and in its courtyard, which was architecturally redesigned in 1929 – is quite extensive and full of fascinating surprises.

Address Piazza Bra 28, 37121 Verona, Tel 0039/045/590087 | **Public Transit** Bus 11, 12, 13, 72, 90, 92, 93, 96, 97, 98, 510 to the Piazza Bra stop | **Hours** Tues–Sun 8:30am–2pm (ticket office closes at 1:15pm) | **Tip** Classical concerts are often held in the neighboring Accademia Filarmonica. The remarkable hall, Baroque in design, has been faithfully restored after sustaining war damage.

87 Palazzo Pompei

Bitten by the natural history bug

The Palazzo Pompei, which today houses the city's natural history museum, gives you an idea of what it was like inside a Renaissance palace.

Construction began in the early 1530s and continued for more than thirty years. Michele Sanmicheli designed the palace at the request of Nicolò Lavezzola. Through marriage, it passed a short time later into the ownership of the Pompei family, who gifted it to the city of Verona in the 19th century.

While the palace now lies lower than it originally did thanks to the riverbank fortifications and corresponding new street, the Lungadige Porta Vittoria, which were built in 1890 after the flood of 1882, its magnificent facade was once an impressive sight along the river.

On the inside, the Palazzo Pompei maintains its original sequence of rooms. The building is entered through the central archway, and the main pathway leads you through a large vestibule, followed by the courtyard, a hall, and the garden, which is adjoined by further rooms. The inner courtyard, flanked by arcades on all sides, is especially beautiful and is alone worth a visit.

Geologic, Stone Age, and botanical specimens are on display in the museum alongside animals, both taxidermied and preserved floating in formalin. Even if the presentation at times can appear somewhat "dusty," there are all sorts of interesting things to discover, such as the huge skull of a whale whose bones recall those at the Arco della Costa (see page 126). The 75-foot-long mammal died in 1973 in a collision with a ship in the Gulf of Genoa, and its skeleton came to Verona thanks to a friendship between the ship's owner and the museum's director.

Also worth seeing are the marble slabs in the rear stairwell. They display the full color spectrum of the stone from the region around Verona and include samples containing fossils.

Address Lungadige Porta Vittoria 9, 37129 Verona, Tel 0039 / 045 / 8079400 | **Public Transit** Bus 11, 12, 13, 51, 90, 92, 98, 510 to the Via XX Settembre stop | **Hours** Mon–Thurs 9am–5pm, Sat and Sun 2–6pm | **Tip** On the riverbank directly across from the museum, you can see the *Dogana*, the historic customs house from the 18th century.

88 Pandoro

The birthplace of the traditional Italian dessert

As you travel down the Corso Porta Borsari from the Piazza delle Erbe, on your left where the Vicolo Corticella San Marco begins, you'll see a brightly plastered palazzo with a very unique decoration. On the balcony of the upper floor, a star-shaped cake, the Pandoro, is immortalized in stone. The old blue neon letters hanging vertically over the street read *Melegatti*, a household name in Verona and beyond.

Melegatti SpA, a wholesale bakery specializing in cakes, is counted among the leading bakeries in all of Italy. Its headquarters are now found in the nearby town of San Giovanni Lupatoto. It's known mostly for the Pandoro, however, whose birth can be traced back to this little shop in Verona. Domenico Melegatti had run a small *pasticceria* right here in the building at Corso Porta Borsari 19–21 since 1894. In this bakery he first created the pastry that would one day make him famous, namely a sweet yeast cake in the shape of a star baked with a fluffy dough made from eggs. The legend goes that a assistent who tasted the cake upon stopping by the bakery enthusiastically exclaimed: *L'è proprio un pan de oro!* ("This really is a bread made of gold!"). The name stuck, and so began the story of its success.

Believing he had succeeded in inventing something truly sensational, the enterprising Melegatti patented his "Pandoro" and presented it to the masses with great success. When imitators tried to pass off their breads as the same as his, Melegatti offered 1,000 lire to anyone who could actually reproduce the true Pandoro recipe. Not one competitor even tried, so unique was the original.

The Pandoro, meanwhile, became the traditional dessert served at Christmas throughout Italy. It is enjoyed on other holidays also, and often is served on Sundays as a *dolce*. At Easter, a special version of the cake is sold, called the *Colomba*, which is made from the same dough in the shape of a dove.

Address Corso Porta Borsari 19–21, 37121 Verona | **Public Transit** Bus 70 to the Piazza Erbe stop; Bus 96, 97 to the Lungadige Rubele stop | **Hours** Not open to the public | **Tip** The small 13th-century church of San Giovanni in Foro located diagonally across the street at Corso Porta Borsari 27, is worth a visit.

89 Pasticceria De Rossi

Tasty tarts and the kisses of Romeo and Juliet

You can see many people in Verona carrying home small, flat packages tied with ribbon. These usually contain the *dolci* and *pasticcini* that are enjoyed with coffee after a sumptuous meal. The Pasticceria De Rossi, located in a beautiful palazzo built in 1572 at the upper end of Corso Porta Borsari on the Piazza delle Erbe, is among the finest purveyors of these sweet little treats. It is nearly impossible to choose among the approximately 120 varieties of pastries available, as each one looks more appetizing than the next. Brothers Fabio and Alessandro De Rossi run the business together, now in its third generation.

Among the sweet little goodies are of course the Baci di Giulietta (kisses of Juliet) and the Baci di Romeo (kisses of Romeo). Originally, there were only Juliet's variety of the chocolate heart-shaped cookies baked from almond paste, but later the vanilla kisses of Romeo also were created. A unique specialty of the house is the Torta Russa, a round cake made of a light dough that uses almond flour in a puff pastry shell. The cake is said to have gotten its name because it resembles a type of Russian fur hat.

De Rossi is not only a pastry shop, but also a bakery in the classical sense. You will find an incredible 70 different types of bread on offer, not to mention focaccia, pizza, and *grissini* (long, thin breadsticks). In addition, the bakery also produces *pasta fresca* ("fresh pasta"), and there are several varieties, from simple linguine to filled pastas like ravioli and tortellini.

The store, in business since 1947, is usually jam-packed with people, and an orderly system of taking a number at the entrance is in place, so bellying up to the counter as you might at other Italian bakeries is avoided. After you've received your items, you proceed to the checkout, where payment is handled separately from the ordering. In this way, the pleasant, white-capped salespeople only touch the goods, not the money.

Address Corso Porta Borsari 3, 37121 Verona | **Public Transit** Bus 70 to the Piazza Erbe stop; Bus 96, 97 to the Lungadige Rubele stop | **Hours** Mon–Sat 8am–7:30pm | **Tip** Savory treats galore, including ham, cheese, and olives, are on offer in the nearby Salumeria G. Albertini, with its beautiful art nouveau storefront at Corso Sant'Anastasia 41.

90__Pescheria

The most historic supermarket in the city

In the center of Verona, few of the beautiful old *alimentari*, the small traditional neighborhood markets, remain. Even the newfangled *supermercato* is a rare find. There is one market located just a few steps away from the Piazza dei Signori, however, that is definitely worth a visit. It is located in the rust-red-colored building adorned with battlements bounding the picturesque little square of Largo Pescheria Vecchia. Formerly it served as the *pescheria*, or fish market, as the central stone panel under the three raised battlements indicates.

The history of the single-story building goes back a long way. In 1468, the city council erected a meat market here and laid out the square in front of it. Considered one of the first Renaissance buildings in Verona, the prestigious structure, within whose walls the community secured a very important part of their diet, was designed in the most current, fashionable style. The rear facade stood right along the west bank of the Adige River, so waste could be disposed of into the water immediately, before any offending odors could build up.

During the great flood of 1882, the building was badly damaged and received in its subsequent reconstruction a new, inwardly offset rear facade, which reduced the building's overall footprint. The three arches on the piazza and the two rows of interior columns supporting the roof beams were retained in the building, however, which was then repurposed as a fish market. As a result of the flood disaster, the city built new reinforcements along the riverbank, and the new road Lungadige Tullio Donatelli was created between the *pescheria* and the Adige.

Strolling along the aisles of the market, with its long modern shelves and huge marble pillars, it's hard to believe that the Veronese people have been doing their grocery shopping in this same building for almost 550 years.

Address Piazzetta Pescheria, 37121 Verona | **Public Transit** Bus 70 to the Piazza Viviani stop; Bus 96, 97 to the Lungadige Rubele stop | **Hours** Mon–Sat 9am–1pm and 4–8 pm, closed Sundays | **Tip** The longstanding specialty shop for knives Coltelleria Calcagni, located at Largo Pescheria Vecchia 3, also offers a variety of c orresponding kitchen appliances.

91__Piazza delle Erbe

Stones drowning in color

Should you find yourself basking in the glorious sunshine one fine day in Verona and suddenly notice that the locals are walking around with umbrellas and raincoats – perhaps even carrying their little dogs bundled up in chic, vibrantly colored waterproof coats – don't stand by in wonder for too long. Steel yourself and take heed. The first glimpse of a cloud in the sky means it's imperative that you hurry and take cover.

The weather can abruptly change here from one minute to the next: downpours coupled with thunderstorms and squalls arrive with unusual violence. The drains and runoff channels can't absorb the vast amount of water pouring down, so the streets become flooded and puddles the size of small ponds form on the sidewalks and pavement. Smoothly polished marble paving stones can quickly turn into a slip 'n' slide for pedestrians. If you're lucky, the city will have recently picked the stones with hoes to provide some traction. On the positive side, walking so slowly over the stones will allow you to marvel at the full spectrum of rich hues that comes alive when they are polished with rainwater. From the familiar off-white to bright salmon pink and from the rust-colored classic *Marmo Rosso di Verona* to the dark hue of mussel shells, the stones seem to glow with an inner intensity.

The Piazza delle Erbe and other squares and streets around the city are quickly swept clear of pedestrians. Many people seek refuge under porticoes and archways, which were built just for these rigors of the weather. The only people remaining on the streets are the merchants selling their wares from pushcarts, who, as lightning fast as the coming of the storm, have replaced the sunglasses on display with a variety of umbrellas. For them, doing good business means acting quickly, as in a matter of minutes it might clear up again, with the sky returning to a bright blue as though nothing at all has happened.

Address Piazza delle Erbe, 37121 Verona | **Public Transit** Bus 70 to the Piazza Erbe stop; Bus 96, 97 to the Lungadige Rubele stop | **Tip** Borsi, a shop located on the corner of Corso Sant'Anastasia and Via Mazzanti, has a good selection of umbrellas on offer.

92__The Picture Gallery

The wooden ceiling in San Fermo Maggiore

It is said that the lovely church of San Fermo Maggiore houses the largest collection of 14th-century art in Verona. But this is not an "art gallery" in the traditional sense. Here, you must look up to view the majority of works on display.

In the upper church, high above your head, long rows of images of saints adorns the extraordinary wooden ceiling. The friezes with tracery arcades are visible when viewed from an angle. Behind the small arches, which function as small windows, you can see the portraits of men and women crowned with halos. Full of life, they have their heads turned in various directions and their robes glow with strong colors.

There are 416 pictures in total, which were executed upon the completion of ceiling construction in 1350. You can't help but feel for the painter, who pursued his work here on scaffolding at dizzying heights. Because his name is not recorded, he's been nicknamed *Maestro del Redentore*, or Master of the Redeemer. The frescoes around the archway at the choir are also his work, or at least that of artists in his workshop.

Towards the top of the arch, near the ceiling, the builder and benefactor are immortalized in donor portraits. On the left, the prior of the Franciscan cloister, Daniele Gusmerio, kneels praying, clearly recognizable as a monk from his tonsure and religious habit. Directly across from him on the right side of the arch is a depiction of Guglielmo di Castelbarco, the patron of the building's construction. Splendidly dressed, he holds a large model of San Fermo Maggiore in his hands. Its facade is immediately recognizable as that of the actual church.

Before leaving, you should be sure to visit the crypt, or lower church. San Fermo Maggiore was built between 1061 and 1143 as a two-story church and the lower church originally served only as a repository for the relics of the holy martyrs Fermo and Rustico.

Address Stradone San Fermo, 37121 Verona | **Public Transit** Bus 11, 12, 13, 51, 73, 90, 92, 98, 510 to the San Fermo stop | **Hours** Mon–Sat 9:30am–6pm, Sun 1–6pm | **Tip** There is a plaque on a house standing nearby at Via Leoncino 14 indicating that the opera singer Maria Callas lived there from 1950 to 1955.

93__The Pigna
Directional help for a complicated street plan

The giant stone *pigna* ("pinecone"), stands on a squat column on the corner of Via Pigna and Via Verità. Finely hewn from marble, the statue dates back to Roman times. It probably originally crowned a gravestone, though nobody knows this for sure. In the Middle Ages, people were already referring to this part of the city as *la pigna* and the name was also given to churches in the area, such as San Giacomo alla Pigna.

This pinecone functions as a sort of compass needle and guides the way for the many visitors strolling through the streets of Verona. The streets of Roman cities were typically laid out with a regular grid pattern, and Verona, too, would have had this regular orientation, were it not for the Adige River. The Romans chose the location for Verona based on its natural topological features, namely the river running in a large arc, which afforded the city military protection from two sides. The Romans fit their customary right-angled street plan into the bend of the Adige, skewing it slightly on the diagonal. Therefore the Decumanus Maximus, the main street of the Roman city whose path is traced today by the Corso Porta Borsari and the Corso Sant'Anastasia, did not run in a straight east-west direction, as was typical in other Roman cities, but rather from southwest to northeast. The Via Pigna ran parallel, and was known to the Romans as the Decumanus Sinistratus, because it was the second route to the left of the Decumanus Maximus (the Latin *sinistratus* means "to the left").

When you find yourself at the street corner where the *pigna* sits, a quick glance at the map makes you realize that there's nothing frustrating about finding your way around the city. Looking down the Via Pigna, you'll see the Adige and the range of hills across the river. Turning 90 degrees to the west, you can go down the Via San Giacomo, the continuation of the Via Verità, and reach the Adige in the same way.

Address Corner of Via Pigna and Via Verità, 37121 Verona | **Public Transit** Bus 70 to the Piazza Duomo stop; Bus 96, 97 to the Lungadige San Giorgio stop | **Tip** From the *pigna*, a short walking path leads through the narrow and historic Via San Giacomo alla Pigna straight to the cathedral.

94_Ponte Pietra
The Roman bridge over the Adige

The name of the Ponte Pietra ("stone bridge") describes its construction. Once known as the Pons Marmoreus, it is the only stone arch bridge in the city of Verona, as well as the only one that dates back to Roman times. When the water level in the Adige river is low, you can see the remaining original pier foundations of a second Roman bridge, the Ponte Postumio.

The Ponte Pietra's two arches closest to the left bank, made of massive marble blocks, are from the bridge's original construction, while the three other brick arches date back to the 1298 repair of the bridge under Alberto I della Scala. At that time there was also a watchtower constructed at the bridgehead. Its counterpart on the other side was dismantled at the beginning of the 19th century, along with numerous wooden structures lining the bridge that housed the apartments of millers and boatswains, stalls, and small businesses.

The Ponte Pietra was the only one of Verona's many bridges to hold up against the flood of 1882. It was not immune to the power of mines, however, and was destroyed by the German troops during their retreat on the evening of April 24, 1945.

Using the stones that were found in the river, the Veronese faithfully reconstructed the bridge in the late 1950s. Today the now pedestrian-only bridge is very popular with the people of Verona because of its location at the top of the bend in the Adige River.

Two openings in the bridge, a large circular hole in the middle and a round-arched "window" between the Roman arches, contribute to its picturesque image. These passages probably served to alleviate the water pressure on the piers in the case of a flood. Today the normal water level of the Adige is much lower than in the past, and the openings act more like peepholes that capture the view from the shore and, depending on your perspective, steer your gaze toward the churches of San Giorgio in Braida and Sant'Anastasia, or one of the city's other landmarks lying in the background.

Address Ponte Pietra, 37121 Verona | **Public Transit** Bus 31, 32, 33, 91, 96, 97 to the Teatro Romano stop | **Tip** The only domed church in Verona, San Giorgio in Braida, on the outer northwest corner of the old fortifications, is reached by a walkway along the left bank of the Adige.

95__Porta Borsari

Magnificent scenery from the time of the Romans

For two millennia, the Porta Borsari has stood in exactly the same location. The city gate still marks the beginning of the site of the former Roman city. The overland route of the Via Postumia led straight to the gate and continued on through, becoming the main thoroughfare of the inner city, the Decumanus Maximus, whose route is still followed today by the Corso Porta Borsari and the Corso Sant'Anastasia.

The Porta Borsari was built around the middle of the 1st century b.c. A hundred years later the decorative facade was added, giving the gate the appearance of a stage backdrop as you walk toward it. Its two rounded arches for entering and exiting the city are framed by pillars supporting triangular pediments. Above these rises a two-story facade featuring rows of arched "windows" through which one can see right through to the sky. The interplay of form elements and the coexistence of twisted and fluted columns has inspired many subsequent architects – for example, Michele Sanmicheli, in his design for the Palazzo Bevilacqua, not far away at Corso Cavour 19.

In Roman times, the gate was called the Porta Iovia, or Gate of Jupiter, because it flanked a temple dedicated to the father of the gods. Roman relics are still visible on some of the houses along the Corso – like the Gorgon head at the corner of Via Valerio Catullo or the gravestone a few steps farther. In the Middle Ages the gate was renamed Porta Borsari, after the *bursarii*, who collected taxes on the goods imported into the city.

Though the gate stood for quite some time amid the hustle and bustle and busy traffic of the city, for a few years now peace has returned. The old city center has been declared a zone with *traffico limitato*. Cars owned by residents, taxis, and electric buses are allowed only on a handful of side streets, allowing pedestrians full use of the entire width of the Corso.

Address Corso Porta Borsari, 37121 Verona | **Public Transit** Bus 21, 22, 23, 24, 31, 32, 33, 41, 42, 61, 62, 91, 94, 95 to the A. Diaz stop | **Tip** If you go through the gate in the direction of Corso Cavour, the home of the Renaissance painter Niccolò Giolfino lies on the left-hand side of the road. He decorated the house with numerous frescoes, some of which are still visible today.

96 Porta dei Bombardieri

The military gateway on the Palazzo del Capitano

You'll know whom this city gate was meant to commemorate the minute you see its Baroque decorations: the *bombardieri*, or artillerymen. Their task was to load and fire the so-called bombards, an early type of cannon that shot stone balls.

The Porta dei Bombardieri is located in the courtyard of the Palazzo del Capitano on the Piazza dei Signori. The Palazzo was built by the Scaligeri ruler Cansignorio and served during Venetian rule as the seat of the Capitano, the top military official in the city. It was his role to keep the city secure and, if necessary, organize its defense. Usually the professional soldiers provided by Venice were insufficient, however, so the Capitano would also draw from the Scuola dei Bombardieri, an artillery school in which civilians were trained and held at the ready.

Citizens were enticed to fill the school's ranks through tax incentives and low-cost housing. Craftsmen and merchants numbered high among the members of the military *scuola*, also known as the Compagna di Santa Barbara, which included the sculptor Bernardino Miglioranzi, who created the gateway in 1687 on behalf of the organization.

The decorations on the gate are practically a weapons museum, depicting the entire arsenal available at the time, including cannons, spears, battle drums, pistols, powder horns, lances, torches, helmets, and shields.

The cannons, which frame the gate like columns, are each adorned with a medallion of Santa Barbara, the patron saint of artillerymen. A bit of the artist's imagination shows through in the combination of all this military equipment, though, as he positioned the heavy cannons atop drums. It is said that the absurdity of this placement, both in structural and contextual terms, earned Bernardino massive amounts of criticism. He was so aggrieved by this that he took his own life, or so goes the rumor that runs around Verona to this day.

Address Piazza dei Signori, 37121 Verona | **Public Transit** Bus 70 to the Piazza Viviani stop; Bus 96, 97 to the Lungadige Rubele stop | **Tip** The entrance to the Scavi Scaligeri, an excavation area that is also used for photography exhibitions, is located in this same courtyard.

97__Porta Nuova & Porta Palio

An impressive first impression of the city

For many visitors, their image of Verona is defined by its massive city gates to the south. From the train station, you'll pass through the Porta Nuova and, coming from the airport or Lake Garda, the Porta Palio. The approach roads lead over the greenbelt and through the archways of the gates, with the fortification walls beyond.

The city wall dates back to the reign of the della Scala family, known as the Scaligeri, from 1260 to 1387. After the Republic of Venice took control of the city in 1405, the fortifications were modernized and strengthened. The decision to build the new gates was made in connection with the War of the League of Cambrai at the beginning of the 16th century.

As the official architect and military engineer for the Republic of Venice, Michele Sanmicheli designed both the Porta Nuova and the Porta Palio. Previously at these locations there had only been insignificant openings in the wall, so these gates became powerful symbolic constructions with a military function. With the Porta Nuova, built between 1533 and 1542, the important road axis to the Piazza Bra was created at the same time. While the elongated portion of the gate facing into the city remained unchanged, the outer facade was originally decorated with marble covering only the middle section. In 1854, during the time of Austrian rule, the side areas were matched to the center accordingly. The Porta Palio, built in the middle of the 16th century, aligned with the second radial road axis, the Stradone Porta Palio.

The emotional effect of the gates today is the same as it was originally. Through their ashlar masonry they appear monumental and indomitable. Modeled after ancient triumphal arches, they lead to a city that was already magnificent in Roman times and celebrated a revival during the Renaissance.

Address Circonvallazione Alfredo Oriani, 37122 Verona | **Public Transit** Main bus station at the Stazione di Verona Porta Nuova (central station) | **Tip** A lovely walking path atop the old fortification walls leads out from the Porta Nuova through the Parco delle Mura.

98 Portoni della Bra

On the trail of Romeo and Juliet

Many portions of the city walls, which were originally built between 1194 to 1224 to secure the built-up area within the bend in the Adige River, remain intact though the wall lost its protective importance once the newer fortress line was built farther south. A city gate with two large arches was opened in these walls at the end of the 15th century, which provided access to the Piazza Bra. The new gate was therefore named the Portoni della Bra.

The gate is bordered on both sides by buildings, to the east by a pentagonal fortified tower and the Palazzo della Gran Guardia and to the west by the Museo Maffeiano (see page 180). The large clocks on both facades, a gift from Count Antonio Nogarola, were installed in 1872.

Attached to the city-facing side near the Museo Maffeiano is a bronze bust of William Shakespeare, which was donated by the Club di Giulietta. On a stone tablet next to the bust, Romeo's desperate words following the death of Tybalt are inscribed in both English and Italian: "There is no world without Verona walls, But purgatory, torture, hell itself. Hence banished is banish'd from the world, And world's exile is death …" In order to help the tourists believe that they are following in the footsteps of the tragedy, it is suggested that Romeo left the city by way of the arches of the Portoni della Bra on his flight to Mantua.

The Club di Giulietta, which was actually founded in 1975 by Giulio Tamassia as a circle of friends for the culturally minded people of the city, now focuses on answering the personal letters addressed to Juliet written by lovers and fans from around the world. A predominantly female team answers the approximately 5,000 letters and 2,000 emails received every year. The 2010 movie *Letters to Juliet*, starring Vanessa Redgrave and Amanda Seyfried, depicted the phenomenon and led the ancient love story to its long-awaited happy ending.

MUSEO LAPIDARIO
MAFFEIANO

THERE IS NO WORLD WITHOVT VERONA WALLS,
BVT PVRGATORY, TORTVRE, HELL ITSELF.
HENCE BANISHED IS BANISH'D FROM THE WORLD,
AND WORLD'S EXILE IS DEATH: . . . . "

NON ESISTE MONDO FVOR DALLE MVRA DI VERONA;
MA SOLO PVRGATORIO, TORTVRA, INFERNO.
CHI È BANDITO DI QVI, È BANDITO DAL MONDO
L'ESILIO DAL MONDO È MORTE; . . . . "

HAKESPEARE, "ROMEO AND JVLIET", ATTO III, SCENA III)

WILLIAM SHAKESPEARE

Address Piazza Bra, 37121 Verona | **Public Transit** Bus 11, 12, 13, 72, 90, 92, 93, 96, 97, 98, 510 to the Piazza Bra stop | **Tip** The Palazzo della Gran Guardia is used for large special exhibitions and also is open for tours.

99__Portrait of a Child with a Drawing

The picture within a picture

The painting created by the Veronese artist Giovan Francesco Caroto around 1520 appears so lifelike that it seems as if it could be a photograph. The representation on the small wooden tablet, which measures only 14.5 by 11.5 inches, speaks directly to visitors of the art gallery in the Museo di Castelvecchio. The redheaded young boy wearing a green jacket is captured at exactly the moment he turns his head toward the viewer. His shoulder-length hair appears to be slightly in motion, still swinging after him, while with bright eyes and a broad smile he proudly holds up his own artwork in his right hand. In the style you'd expect of a child, his drawing portrays a stick figure with long, thin arms and legs. Upon closer examination, however, there are two details to note on the right side of his sheet of paper. As though he were working in an almost professional manner, the little master has first practiced his sketches. They depict a portion of a face, with the well-defined arch from the nose to the eyebrow, as well as a separate eye in profile with detailed lid and lashes.

The visual theme of the painting is unique. Just as the boy presents his drawing of a person, perhaps even of himself, Giovan Francesco Caroto presents a portrait of the child to the viewer. It is a snapshot of a moment that captures the subject's state of mind with a remarkable directness. Art historians suspect that the work is the Veronese painter's attempt to echo the style of Leornardo da Vinci, whose own works he became familiar with during visits to Milan.

The portrait raises many questions, but the intense gaze of the child repeated in the small sketches of the eye seem above all to want to convey one thing: namely to "truly" see and to perceive that decisive moment in which someone reveals more than just what can be seen from the outside.

Address Corso Castelvecchio 2, 37121 Verona, Tel 0039/045/8062611 | **Public Transit** Bus 21, 22, 23, 24, 31, 32, 33, 41, 42, 61, 62, 91, 94, 95 to the Corso Castelvecchio stop | **Hours** Tues–Sun 8:30am–7:30pm, Mon 1:30–7:30pm (ticket office closes at 6:45pm) | **Tip** Take a look into the now dry moat of the Castelvecchio, and you'll recognize that stone blocks from the Arena were used in the construction of its foundation.

100 Putti Friezes

Historic advertising on the city's buildings

While walking through the streets of Verona, you should keep your gaze directed upward toward the tops of the walls just under the eaves of the buildings. There are often still beautiful paintings and frescoes to discover on the upper portions of the buildings' facades. Many of these decorations have been preserved well over time thanks to the protection from rain and wind provided by the wide overhanging roofs.

Well into the 19th century, the city was famous for its wealth of painted facades, and was sometimes referred to as the *città dipinta*, or painted city. Many of these have since been lost due to weathering, destruction, or renovation. Some earlier inventories of the painted works, such as that of the German art historian Gunter Schweikhart, give an overall impression of the former face of the city. The paintings often had mythological or biblical themes, and contained political innuendo or moral statements. In other cases, they alluded to the profession of the building's owner and its function.

The plaster is crumbling off the facade of the house at Via Ponte di Pietra 23–25, but under the eaves you can still see the painted frieze. Even from a distance, you can recognize putti diligently pursuing various activities. They steer a horse-drawn carriage, lug dried fish suspended from sticks, and slaughter a pig. A grocer apparently had his business in this house.

On the palazzo at Via Pigna 14 you can see a similar putti frieze on the high wall, which probably also originates from the first half of the 16th century. In five light gray frames, the small figures are seen working with sacks, chests, and bales of cloth, and leading a goat. This homeowner was evidently employed in some way in the cloth industry, an important branch of the Veronese economy, and the elaborate painting here also served to advertise the owner's business.

Address Palazzo Zignoni: Via Ponte di Pietra 23–25, Palazzo: Via Pigna 14, 37121 Verona | **Public Transit** Bus 70 to the Piazza Duomo stop; Bus 96, 97 to the Lungadige San Giorgio stop | **Tip** An inscription on the building at the corner of the Piazza Broilo and Via Ponte di Pietra claims that scorpion oil was once manufactured there as a medicinal remedy according to the recipe of the *medico "perfettissimo"* Pietro Andrea Mattiolo.

101_A Saintly Stone
The legend of San Zeno in Oratorio

A huge stone, polished smooth over thousands of years by the forces of nature, is on display in the small church of San Zeno in Oratorio. On a marble tablet in the wall behind the stone, a Latin inscription explains its significance: *Hoc super incumbens saxo prope fum(i)nis undam Zeno pater tremula captabat a rundine pisces.* "On this piece of rock, which floated on a wave of the river, Father Zeno caught fish with a switch from an Aspen tree." According to legend, this rock, which sat in the Adige River, was the favorite spot of the revered local saint who is said to have converted the Veronese to Christianity. Again and again he came to the riverfront for fishing and soul searching, and around 1,650 years ago, you would have found him sitting on this very stone.

Even from today's perspective, you can well understand the reason San Zeno sought out this idyllic little spot along a bend in the river to pass his leisure time. In the 12th century, the Romanesque church, which the Veronese will often refer to in the diminutive, *San Zenetto*, was built on the same spot.

You enter the forecourt of the church from a small side street off of the Regaste San Zeno. The brick facade that you see today is not the original one, however. Under Napoleon, San Zeno in Oratorio was badly damaged and eventually shut down. During restoration work in the 19th century, architectural elements from other destroyed churches were repurposed, such as the Romanesque vestibule, the Gothic windows on its sides, and the rose window. The three-nave interior with its open timbering, though, retains its original shape and atmosphere.

An antique treasure serves as the base for the saint's stone. The cylindrical tomb dating from the 1st century A.D. shows two busts in an ornate framing, probably the portrait of a married couple. Other finds nearby suggest that there was very likely a cemetery here in Roman times.

Address Vicolo San Zeno in Oratorio 2–4, 37123 Verona | **Public Transit** Bus 31 to the Regaste S. Zeno stop; Bus 21, 22, 23, 24, 32, 33, 41, 42, 61, 62, 91, 94, 95 to the Corso Castelvecchio stop | **Hours** Generally open daily | **Tip** A lovely walking path leads from here along the Adige to the area of the Basilica of San Zeno Maggiore.

102__ Santa Rita da Cascia
A saint for all seasons

If you see a stream of women with roses in their hands running through the streets of Verona one morning, you'll know that it must be May 22, the feast day of Saint Rita of Cascia. In the small church of Santa Maria Antica near the Scaliger Tombs, a relic of the saint is preserved and there is a wooden sculpture depicting her in the niche to the left of the altar. In orderly rows, countless votive hearts have been hung in gratitude for support and help granted by the saint, as Rita is invoked primarily by women with unsolvable problems and in desperate situations. In 1900, she was canonized by Pope Leo XIII as *la Santa degli Impossibili*, the saint of impossible causes.

The saint's feast day is celebrated on the anniversary of the day in 1457 when Rita is said to have died in the Augustinian convent in the Umbrian town of Cascia. Several masses are now heard annually in the church of Santa Maria Antica. At the end of each service there is always a consecration of the roses brought to mass by the celebrants, and the container housing the relic may be touched and kissed. The roses are then dried at home and stored until the following year. And should one of your friends find herself in a difficult situation without a miraculous Rita rose of her own, you can simply pull a petal off of yours to give to her.

The wooden figure represents the legend according to which Rita is said to have experienced stigmata in a vision: a thorn from the crown worn by Christ was drilled into her forehead and left a wound that lasted for many years. Before her death, the saint asked that a rose be brought to her from the cloister's garden, and though the temperatures outside were freezing, nonetheless a rosebush was in full bloom.

Her veneration spread rapidly throughout Italy through further miracles, so that in local folk piety, Rita stands right after Saint Anthony among the most important of the saints.

Address Via Arche Scaligere 3, 37121 Verona | Public Transit Bus 70 to the Piazza Viviani stop; Bus 96, 97 to the Lungadige Rubele stop | Hours Generally open daily | Tip The Basilica of San Zeno Maggiore and San Fermo sport roofs similar to the conical, red tiled one atop Santa Maria Antica's Romanesque campanile.

103 — Scaligeri Fortifications

A stroll through the hills

The crenellated ramparts on the hills that surround Verona in an arc from north to east can be seen from many points throughout the city. They were built as protective fortifications under the Scaligeri ruler Cangrande I in the 1320s, greatly expanding the original Roman city footprint to include tracts of land to the west and the east. The walls were modified and strengthened in 1520 by the Venetians, and again by the Austrians in 1830 in accordance with the latest military technology.

Along the inside of the walls runs a footpath, ideal and inviting for a contemplative walk away from the urban hustle and bustle of the city below. It will take you a good half hour to travel from the most northerly point at the gate behind the Castel San Pietro over to the Porta Vescovo in the east. You can also get there from one of the small streets leading up into the hills from Veronetta, such as Via San Zeno in Monte.

From up close, the view of the fortifications is no less impressive than from afar. The walls were built using the tuff stone that was dug up during the construction of the trench on the other side. Rows of rough-hewn stones alternate with equal layers of fill material up to a height of nearly twenty feet, and the crenellated battlements follow in regular intervals. Brackets still indicate where there was originally a walkway attached to the imposing walls. There are also fourteen towers, where the masonry was once clad in brick, which is still noticeable today.

The 700-year-old wall still marks the city limits. New buildings with multi-family dwellings reach up to this point. From one of the many ancient archways in the wall, however, you have an unobstructed view out to the countryside, with the overgrown moat and supplementary fortress buildings from later periods tapering off into the sparsely populated rural foothills of the majestic Lessini Mountains.

Address Via San Zeno in Monte, 37129 Verona | **Public Transit** Bus 31, 32, 33, 91, 96, 97 to the Teatro Romano stop | **Tip** Near the Porta Vescovo lies the church of San Nazaro e Celso, which contains frescoes and paintings by famous Veronese Renaissance artists that are worth seeing.

104_ The Statue of San Zeno
The laughing bishop

The statue of San Zeno appears friendly and happy to visitors of his church. The Veronese themselves speak of *San Zen che ride* ("San Zeno, who laughs"). Just as noticeable as the smiling visage in the lifelike rendering of the patron saint of Verona, however, is his dark complexion, for San Zeno, who served as the eighth bishop of Verona, from about 362 to 380, is believed to have been of North African descent and probably came from Mauritania.

The figure, made from marble, is located in the niche of the northern staircase leading up to the high choir box. A local artist created the likeness during the 13th century. Seated on a throne and raising his right hand in a blessing, San Zeno is identifiable as a bishop through his papal red robe, pallium, and miter and staff. From the crook of his bishopric staff hangs a fish, in reference to the legend according to which Zeno supported himself by fishing in the Adige River. For this reason, he is also regarded as the patron saint of freshwater fishing.

Through various miracles Zeno came to be revered as a saint even during his lifetime. In the 9th century, a small church was built on the site of his grave in a Roman-Early Christian cemetery. In its place now stands the much larger Basilica of San Zeno Maggiore. Built between 1120 and 1138, it is a masterpiece of Romanesque architecture in Italy and popular destination for many visitors to Verona. The chruch underwent further renovations and additions in the centuries that followed.

San Zeno, whose remains were reburied in 807 and are now kept in an urn in the apse of the cathedral, can be found pictured in other works of art around the building. On the famous San Zeno altarpiece, Renaissance painter Andrea Mantegna in 1541 depicted the saint with a black beard and bishopric insignia. Also on the bronze doors, which date from the late 11th century, the life of the revered San Zeno is represented on four panels.

Address Piazza S. Zeno, 37123 Verona | **Public Transit** Bus 31, 32, 33 to the Piazza Pozza stop; Bus 61, 93 to the Via Da Vico stop | **Hours** 8:30am–6pm, Sun 1–6pm | **Tip** A vestibule supported by two columns resting atop lions adorns the cathedral's facade.

105_ Teatro Romano

An outdoor stage with wide views over the city

Not only does Verona have an amphitheater, the Arena, that dates back to Roman times, but also a wonderful theater. The Roman theater was built taking advantage of the topography of a hill on the left bank of the Adige River, and was laid out in the typically ideal shape, consisting of a semicircle with tiered seating all oriented toward a stage on the straight side.

If you picture in your mind that the Roman city at the time of the theater's construction in the first century B.C. lay completely across from the building site within the bend in the Adige, the placement of the theater on a prominent point on the other side of that bend must have had great significance. Not only did the rows of seats stagger up the hill concentrically in two terraces to a height of nearly 200 feet, but the theater was also crowned with a temple up at the very top of the hill.

Were it not for a wealthy and energetic Veronese merchant in the 19th century, we would probably not be able to see the theater today. The complex, which over the centuries had fallen into disrepair, had been completely built over when Andrea Monga bought the site. He had the many small houses constructed on top of it destroyed, sparing only the convent of San Girolamo and the church of Santi Siro e Libera, and then carried out extensive excavations. In 1904 the city of Verona acquired the site and continued the excavation work to the point that it's now possible to once again get an idea of the original layout of the theater.

The open-air stage is used from spring to autumn for various events, such as theater performances, concerts, and film screenings. In ancient times, the theater was an enclosed building with a high stage wall running down to the riverbank. It's a great benefit to today's event goers that this wall no longer exists, as the city skyline across the Adige with the Ponte Pietra off to the right now becomes the backdrop to the stage.

Address Regaste Redentore 2, 37129 Verona | **Public Transit** Bus 31, 32, 33, 91, 96, 97 to the Teatro Romano stop | **Hours** Tues–Sun 8:30am–7:30pm, Mon 1:30–7:30pm (ticket office closes at 6:45pm) | **Tip** The archeological museum, which is located in the former convent of San Girolamo, displays Roman archeological finds such as a floor mosaic depicting gladiators.

106_ Torre del Gardello

The first public clock in Verona

The Torre del Gardello looms over 144 feet high next to Palazzo Maffei along the Piazza delle Erbe. The simple brick tower is hardly given any attention, though, given the competition it receives from the richly decorated Baroque facade of the palazzo. Just like the Torre dei Lamberti across town, it is a family-built tower so typical of the Italian Middle Ages.

The inscription on a plaque informs visitors of the tower's special significance and history. It says that it was from the Torre del Gardello, which was erected under the rule of Cansignorio della Scala, and that the first clock bells rang out in Verona in 1370. Those facts are a bit misleading, however, because the tower actually dates from the 12th century and was only repaired and heightened by the Scaligeri ruler.

When work was completed in 1379, a bell that struck the hour was then hung in the tower. For the first time, with this bell, the events and economic life in Verona were regulated and subjected to the time of day. It was one of the earliest striking clocks in the entire world.

The star-shaped clock face was added to the tower in 1421, which made it possible to read the exact time. By this point, the tower was no longer referred to by the name of the family who owned it, but as *il torre dell'orologio*, the clock tower. In 1626, the tower's height was increased by thirteen feet and finished with the crenellated cornice and its peculiar peak. Through the open arches in the new belfry, the chiming of the clock carried to every corner of the growing city. The bells performed their duty until the year 1661, when their internal mechanics broke down irreparably.

The huge bronze bells, with their 36 quintals and diameter greater than four feet, were cast in 1370 by the important bell founder Magister Jacobus. Today they are one of the main exhibits on display at the Museo di Castelvecchio.

Address Corso Porta Borsari / Piazza delle Erbe, 37121 Verona | **Public Transit** Bus 70 to the Piazza Erbe stop; Bus 96, 97 to the Lungadige Rubele stop | **Tip** A kiosk, typical to Verona and Italy as a whole, is found in front of the Torre del Gardello, where you can buy newspapers and magazines.

107 __ Torre dei Lamberti
The view from the top

"See and be seen" should truly be the motto of the Torre dei Lamberti. The top of this 272-foot tower commands an impressive view out over the region; and because of its height, Verona's tallest tower can be seen from nearly all corners of the city.

The Torre dei Lamberti dates from 1172 and was originally constructed as part of the private palazzo of the Lamberti family. Between 1183 and 1194, the Palazzo del Comune (known today as the Palazzo della Ragione), Verona's city hall complex, was built on the same spot, and the existing square tower was integrated into its construction. The white marble octagonal peak of the tower you see today dates from 1463; the original spire was destroyed by lightning during a storm in 1403. In the 15th century, two bells were added (called the "Rengo" and the "Marangone"), one to warn of an impending attack or announce a city council meeting, and the other to alert the city in case of a fire. The tower's huge clock, which watches over Piazza delle Erbe, was only added in 1779.

Visitors can reach the upper belfry by climbing an iron staircase, containing exactly 368 steps, which runs along the inside of the tower's walls. Those who are less athletically inclined can opt instead to take the very modern elevator that was installed in the tower's interior, but will still need to climb an additional 46 steps to reach the top of the first belfry, where tripartite arches on all four sides provide wonderful 360-degree views of the city.

Those really looking for a workout can climb higher up a further 79 winding steps to the zenith of the bell tower. Be forewarned that this final ascent truly can be vertigo inducing – the stairway has no risers, so climbers are constantly forced to look down into the deep tower shaft. It's also a good idea to keep one eye trained on the large clock. You wouldn't want to fall backward from surprise when it chimes on the hour or half hour. The view from the tower's highest point, however, simply can't be topped.

Address Via della Costa 1, 37121 Verona | **Public Transit** Bus 70 to the Piazza Erbe stop; Bus 96, 97 to the Lungadige Rubele stop | **Hours** Tues–Sun 9:30am–7:30pm, Mon 1:45–7:30pm (Ticket office closes at 7pm) | **Tip** Across from the Palazzo della Ragione on the Piazza delle Erbe stand several tall, narrow houses, intended to serve as the ghetto for Verona's Jewish population starting in 1598.

108__ Trattoria Al Pompiere

Veronese specialties in the heart of the city

The nearly square dining room of the Trattoria Al Pompiere, with its old wood-beamed ceiling and checkered tablecloths, looks both comfortable and stylish at the same time. A restaurant has been in this location on the Vicolo Regina D'Ungheria, an alley that branches off from the Via Cappello, for nearly a century. Since 2000, the Al Pompiere has continued the tradition.

The owner and chef, Marco Dandrea, immediately recognizable by his high chef's hat, gladly visits the dining room to make recommendations for his 50 or so guests, as long as he is not needed in the kitchen. In nice weather, a small outdoor patio also is opened up for seating.

Their impressive offerings of *salumi* for an antipasto are sliced to order by a chef near the rear wall of the room. The extensive supply of hams and sausages hanging enticingly from the ceiling seems guaranteed to include anything your heart may desire. The broad selection ranges from hams, bacon, and lardo to various types of salami. There are six kinds of *prosciutto crudo* on offer alone. It is recommended you order a mixed plate and compare the flavors as they melt in your mouth – for example, how the nuances of a *prosciutto crudo veneto* contrast with ham specialties such as *culaccia* or the *culatello di Zibello*.

The rest of the menu features the local cuisine of Verona and the surrounding region and offers high quality and great variety through the inclusion of seasonal produce. The credo of the chef applies to the entire menu: above all, a dish should be *semplice* ("simple"), but not *banale* ("boring").

Locals are also frequent partakers in the lively, warm atmosphere, influenced by the artistic wood-framed portraits that line the walls. These black-and-white images are from the collection of two local photographers, the Bassotto brothers, and depict Veronese personalities from different historical periods.

Address Vicolo Regina D'Ungheria 5, 37121 Verona, Tel 0039 / 045 / 8030537, alpompiere@yahoo.it | **Public Transit** Bus 70 to the Piazza Erbe stop; Bus 96, 97 to the Lungadige Rubele stop | **Hours** Daily, 12:30–2pm and 7:30–10:30pm | **Tip** An offshoot with the same name specializing in sweets and ice creams recently opened on the left bank of the Adige at Via Fontanelle Santo Stefano 10.

109__Valerio Catullo Airport
A walk over the tarmac

Several roads lead to Verona, and besides highway and train connections, air traffic into the city has increased dramatically over the last ten years. The Verona airport was proud to announce in 2006 that it had surpassed the 3-million-passenger mark, and has continued to do so every year since.

The *aeroporto* is named in honor of the Verona-born Roman poet Valerio Catullo, known as Catullus, who lived from circa 84 B.C. to 54 B.C. It was originally a military airport dating back to World War I, and was first opened up to civil aviation in the 1960s. The military area lay on the western side of the site, and the area for private and commercial air passengers across the main runway on the eastern side. However, no active military units have been permanently stationed there since the 1990s.

The airport is located in the town of Villafranca, about eight miles southwest of Verona and just 13 miles from Lake Garda. Flying into the airport on a nice day affords a bird's-eye view of the city's special geographical location. The normal flight path brings you in over the Alps and Lake Garda. Monte Baldo is visible, perhaps still capped with snow, and after a final glimpse of Sirmione and its easily recognizable peninsula, the plane finally turns in the direction of Villafranca.

Though the airport now bustles with flights arriving from all over the world, landing here is still a soothing, tranquil experience. The terminal buildings were recently renovated – the arrivals hall in 2006 and the departure gates in 2011. Even with these upgrades, however, many disembarking passengers must still cross the tarmac on foot to reach the terminal – a special treat that allows you to breathe in the fresh Veronese air with each step and take in the view of the beaurtiful surrounding countryside and the Lessini Mountains in the distance; a welcome first impression of this great city's environs.

Address Aeroporto Valerio Catullo di Verona, Piazzale Aeroporto 1, 37069 Villafranca | **Public Transit** The Aerobus runs between the Stazione di Verona Porta Nuova (the central station) and the airport at 5:15am and then every 20 minutes from 6:10am to 11:10pm. | **Tip** An exhibit in the nearby Museo Nicolis, on the Viale Postumia, displays numerous pieces on the development of automobiles, technology, and mechanics of the last two centuries.

110_ Verona Bike
Exploring the city on two wheels

Mention of the bustling city traffic in Italy usually conjures up a picture of a noisy street teeming with small Fiats and scooters rather than one full of bicycles, but the situation in the center of Verona is quite different.

Here, the bicycle, lovingly called *bici* by the Italians – a shortening of *bicicletta* – is a vital means of transportation. Since the city center is now closed to thru traffic and only buses and resident-owned cars are allowed to drive on certain streets, special bicycle lanes aren't necessary. It's commonplace for residents of the city to use their bikes to run their errands and commute to work each morning.

Verona Bike, a bicycle-sharing system similar to those now found in many cities in Europe and in the United States and throughout Europe, was organized in 2012 by the city government and is run by a private company. You can rent a bike to explore the city directly at the Porta Nuova train station or at one of the other 20 key locations around town affording better access to attractions located outside of the city center. The year-round service allows anyone to rent one of their custom three-geared bikes daily from 6am to midnight for two Euros per day or 25 Euros annually.

The service is not only geared toward tourists, but also locals, in an effort to bolster the use of this environmentally friendly means of transport and keep as many cars off of the city streets as possible. Organizers hope that many people will use the bikes to get to know the historic center of Verona, named to the UNESCO list of World Heritage sites in 2000.

The city center of Verona is compact enough to comfortably wander through its streets by foot, but if you're strapped for time, a bike explores the sights much more efficiently. Because there are no designated bike routes, though, it's especially handy to keep a city map with you.

Address Verona Bike–Front Office, Via degli Alpini 9, 37121 Verona, www.bikeverona.it | **Public Transit** Bus 11, 12, 13, 72, 90, 92, 93, 96, 97, 98, 510 to the Piazza Bra stop | **Hours** Mon–Sat 9am–7pm, Sun 10am–4pm. The call center for Verona Bike is open Mon–Sun 6am–midnight at Tel 800/896948. | **Tip** A ride along the green spaces of the old city walls encircling the entire historic center is a particularly beautiful way to tour Verona.

111_ Via Seghe San Tomaso

Street names reminiscent of the old cityscape

Picture the Adige River flowing placidly, lined with simple buildings and a few palazzos, their walls standing as far out as the waterline. Rowboats and barges float on the river, and a host of mills are anchored fast in the ground, reaching out to the banks over boardwalks. The famous painter Bernardo Bellotto (ca.1721–1780) provides us with this idyllic image of Verona in his three detailed cityscapes from the middle of the 18th century.

Today, however, that tranquil scene is hardly imaginable. The appearance of the city and its riverfront were drastically changed by the flood of 1882. Particularly heavy rainfalls and the melting of the first snows in the Alps that September fueled the continuing rise in the water level of the Adige. First, mills were ripped from their chains by the strong current; one even smashed against the Ponte Nuovo and caused the bridge to collapse. Then, between the 17th and 20th of September, a huge tidal wave poured over two-thirds of Verona.

Wide swaths of the city within the bend of the Adige were flooded, including the San Zeno and Veronetta neighborhoods, which lie directly along the river. Many houses collapsed or were severely damaged. The riverfront underwent a total transformation in the immediate aftermath of the flooding, as the entire length of the Adige's banks were secured by high walls.

Today those places that were destroyed along an old tributary of the Adige in Veronetta are remembered in the new names and layout of the streets. Interrato Dell'Acqua Morta, translated into English roughly as "dead waterway backfilled with soil," is the name of the curved road that traces the old tributary. The present-day Piazza Isolo is named for the island that once lay in the Adige, now connected to the shores through landfill. And those many sawmills, or *seghe*, that were once powered by the flow of the water, remain alive in the name Via Seghe San Tomaso.

Address Via Seghe San Tomaso / Interrato Dell'Aqqua Morta, 37129 Verona | **Public Transit** Bus 31, 32, 33, 73, 91, 96, 97 to the Piazza Isolo stop | **Tip** Some signposts on the Piazza Isolo display historic photographs of the area before the flood.

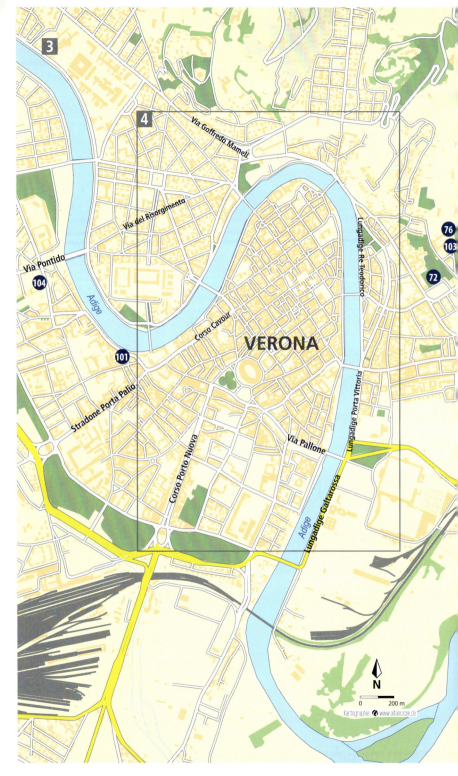

Lucia Jay von Seldeneck,
Carolin Huder, Verena Eidel
**111 PLACES IN BERLIN
THAT YOU SHOULDN'T MISS**
ISBN 978-3-95451-208-9

Rüdiger Liedtke
**111 PLACES IN MUNICH
THAT YOU SHOULDN'T MISS**
ISBN 978-3-95451-222-5

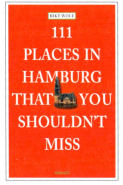

Rike Wolf
**111 PLACES IN HAMBURG
THAT YOU SHOULDN'T MISS**
ISBN 978-3-95451-234-8

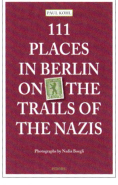

Paul Kohl
**111 PLACES IN BERLIN
ON THE TRAIL OF THE NAZIS**
ISBN 978-3-95451-323-9

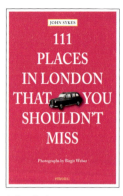

John Sykes
**111 PLACES IN LONDON
THAT YOU SHOULDN'T MISS**
ISBN 978-3-95451-346-8

Dirk Engelhardt
**111 PLACES IN BARCELONA
THAT YOU MUST NOT MISS**
ISBN 978-3-95451-353-6

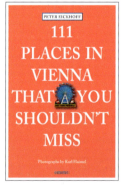

Peter Eickhoff
**111 PLACES IN VIENNA
THAT YOU SHOULDN'T MISS**
ISBN 978-3-95451-206-5

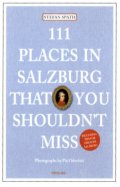

Stefan Spath
**111 PLACES IN SALZBURG
THAT YOU SHOULDN'T MISS**
ISBN 978-3-95451-230-0

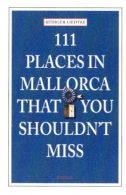

Rüdiger Liedtke
111 PLACES ON MALLORCA
THAT YOU SHOULDN'T MISS
ISBN 978-3-95451-281-2

Marcus X. Schmid
111 PLACES IN ISTANBUL
THAT YOU MUST NOT MISS
ISBN 978-3-95451-423-6

Ralf Nestmeyer
111 PLACES IN PROVENCE
THAT YOU MUST NOT MISS
ISBN 978-3-95451-422-9

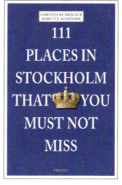

Christiane Bröcker,
Babette Schröder
111 PLACES IN STOCKHOLM
THAT YOU MUST NOT MISS
ISBN 978-3-95451-459-5

About the Author

Petra Sophia Zimmerman, born in 1962 in Bonn, is the author of several scholarly works and also serves as an adjunct professor of art history at the Fachhochschule in Cologne. Petra Sophia's great enthusiasm for Verona took hold while spending time there writing her doctoral thesis. Since then, she has traveled regularly to Verona and Lake Garda, and with the publication of this book, enjoys bringing readers along with her to this very special place.
www.petra-sophia-zimmermann.de